BEE TIGER

The Death's Head Hawk-moth through the Looking-glass

Philip Howse

Brambleby Books

A CIP catalogue record for this book is available from the
British Library.

ISBN 978 1 90824 1627

Cover design Tanya Warren, Creatix
Moth photo on front cover © Alexander Hyde
Design by S4Carisle, www.s4carlisle.com
Photos © Philip Howse unless otherwise stated in figure legends.

Published 2021 by Brambleby Books, UK
www.bramblebybooks.co.uk

Printed and bound by FINIDR, Czech Rep.
FSC and PFSC accredited.

To my wonderful daughters, Debbie and Frances

Le seul véritable voyage, le seul bain de Jouvence, ce ne serait pas d'aller vers de nouveaux paysages, mais d'avoir d'autres yeux, de voir l'univers avec les yeux d'un autre, de cent autres, de voir les cent univers que chacun d'eux voit, que chacun d'eux est.

Marcel Proust

The living pulse of subjective experience cannot finally be stripped from the things that we study (in order to expose the pure unadulterated 'objects') without the things themselves losing all existence for us.

David Abram:
The Spell of the Sensuous

And there aren't any lines in space, so you could join the bits of Orion to bits of Lepus or Taurus or Gemini and say they were a constellation called the Bunch of Grapes or Jesus or The Bicycle (except that they didn't have bicycles in Roman and Greek times which is when they called Orion Orion).

Marc Haddon:
The Curious Incident of the Dog in the Night-time

Our approach to reality, our sense of reality, cannot assume that the text of nature, the book of life, is a cryptogram concealing just a single meaning. Rather, it is an expanding riddle of a multiplicity of resonating images.

Peter Redgrove:
The Black Goddess and the Unseen Real

One day it will have to be officially admitted that what we have christened reality is an even greater illusion than the world of dreams.
Salvador Dalí

There is a theory which states that if ever anyone discovers exactly what the Universe is for and why it is here, it will instantly disappear and be replaced by something even more bizarre and inexplicable. There is another theory which states that this has already happened.
Douglas N. Adams:
The Hitchhiker's Guide to the Galaxy

AUTHOR'S PREFACE

The mysterious and intimidating skull and crossbones markings on the death's head hawk-moth have previously defied rational interpretation. I have here attempted to show how the explanation for them rests on how we and other animals see it. This magnificent insect can be perceived in many different ways – by biologists, non-scientists, artists, superstitious people, birds, bees and bats. Why select the three latter? The death's head is a creature designed to deceive its main predators, which are birds and bats, and it robs bees of their honey without getting stung, again by deceiving them about its true nature. It is able to do all this because of the obvious, but usually overlooked fact that other animals live in a different sensory world to us – their perception is different.

We also tend to ignore the fact that what each person's perceptions are, 'bound by the senses five', as William Blake put it, and furthermore the boundaries may be different from one individual to the next: if you are not colour-blind, for example, it can be difficult to imagine what it is like to be so, and *vice versa*. A very few people can see ultraviolet (UV) light, and some can hear ultrasound up to six times the normal upper limit of human hearing. And some people have synaesthesia (overlap of the senses), seeing colours, for example, when they hear music or read words. It was fascinating also for me to discover that many others cannot tolerate ambiguity or face the possibility that there may be more than one way of interpreting the evidence of their senses; a factor which affects not only their visual perception of a butterfly or moth, but also their attitudes to politics and religion.

I am indebted to Simon Barnes, whose nature writing is an inspiration to me, for his encouragement to embark upon this book. I also here express my thanks to Patric Morrissey, Charles Foster, Andrew Rutherford, James Hamilton-Paterson, David Abram and Clive Farrell for their comments on the draft. Thanks also to Michael Vickers, former Curator of the Ashmolean Museum, who kindly answered some of my questions about the Gorgon Medusa, and Martin Rose for discussions on tolerance of ambiguity – and last, not least to my wife Susan for cheerfully tolerating my obsessions with Lepidoptera. Particular thanks are due to Hugh and Nicola Loxdale for their encouragement and perseverance with the production of this book and for the meticulous editing.

As a prescript, thanks to the poet William Blake for pointing out percipiently that:

He's a Blockhead who wants proof of what he can't perceive
And he's a fool who tries to make such a Blockhead believe.

CONTENTS

FOREWORD

The 1960s saw the death of reality. Certainly of reality as an objective concept. I should know: after all, I was the walrus, I danced beneath a diamond sky with one hand waving free, I saw the Krishna colours on the wall and I knew that logic and proportion had fallen sloppy dead.

It was blindingly – or perhaps eye-openingly – obvious that you and I are entitled to see the world differently: that reality depends on the way you happen to be looking at things at the time. A popular joke of the time: reality is a cop-out for people who can't handle drugs.

And if the ideals of the high period of hippiedom have subsequently fallen into discredit – love and peace and so forth – what has survived is the notion that reality is protean and that seeing is a deeply personal matter. It is a small step to expand this to include other species: creatures with senses and brains by no means identical to our own.

Most birds see in four colours, we humans and our fellow primates see in three, most other mammals in two. No one is wrong: humans just live in a different visual world to blue tits and mice. We traditionally accept that ours is the only way things can be perceived – but with a potent mixture of deep scientific knowledge and powerful visual imagination. Philip Howse has taken us beyond the limits of human perception.

Philip is an academic who has gone rogue. In later life, no longer dependent on the goodwill of colleagues with more orthodox minds, he has gone public with his singular vision of the way life works: the way non-human predators perceive butterflies and moths and the way that butterflies and moths have responded.

We understand life better by studying the living: and that truth is at the heart of what Philip does. Display cabinets and drawings in a field guide are helpful to humans: but in the real world insects move and react and hide. You see them upside down, sideways on, wings in motion, attempting to startle: and that changes everything.

Philip has cracked the code and explained to us why butterflies and moths look as they do. In this fine and thrillingly brief work, he brings the same set of perceptions to the wondrously enigmatic death's head hawk-moth and solves the mystery of why it bears the image of a skull. Along the way he quotes Blake, Proust, Tom Lehrer, Lewis Carroll and Jonathan Agnew, the cricket commentator: an almost unimprovable mixture.

Oh –one point should be cleared up before we go on. I once asked Philip how deep an acquaintance he had with the psychedelic drugs that seemed so important in the 1960s. The answer, surprisingly, was absolutely none whatsoever. I was at first surprised, but later thought – well, just as well. If that's how he sees the world straight, Lord knows what LSD would have done to that excellent brain.

Simon Barnes

INTRODUCTION

Human ingenuity … will never devise anything more beautiful, more simple, or more to the purpose than nature does, because in her inventions nothing is lacking and nothing is superfluous.

Leonardo da Vinci (1452–1519)

Many years ago, on a hot summer's day in the nature reserve of La Tour du Valat in the French Camargue, while I was idly searching the leaves for caterpillars, a death's head hawk-moth fell out of an oak tree at my feet. These wetlands in the Bouches-du-Rhône are notorious for their ravenous mosquitoes, and an area near to the reserve had been routinely sprayed with pesticide as a control measure. The moth had apparently got in the way. This hawk-moth is the second largest moth in Western Europe. The largest is the great peacock moth with a prominent peacock eye on each wing, but the death's head is no less impressive. It has bright yellow underwings and body and a fearsome reputation amongst country folk because of the weird skull-like marking on its thorax: it is regarded as an omen of impending doom with the magical powers of a dragon (Fig. 1). For me at that time it was an omen also, but a favourable one, that changed the course of my research, because from that point on I began to focus on the meanings of the colours and patterns of butterflies and moths.

The 'skull' marking has been a perpetual curiosity for biologists. A. N. Wilson (2017) records in his iconoclastic biography of Charles Darwin (1809–82) that, while an undergraduate at Cambridge, Charles gave his father a death's head hawk-moth for Christmas. This was received by his father, apparently, with admiration for the originality of this gift, although it seems that Charles did not see anything ironical in this. The current attitude amongst many biologists has been that this image is as meaningless as a splattered inkblot that might appear to suggest certain familiar objects. But I have always found it hard to believe this simple explanation for the skull and crossbones image.

Before Charles Darwin, many people accepted the view that living organisms were designed by God and their features were there for a purpose, be it only to amuse us, if nothing else. After he published *The Origin of Species* in 1859, most people came to accept that organisms were fashioned by the unseeing eye of natural selection. Later, when biologists found that survival was dependent upon selection of individuals with genes that carried certain defined benefits for the organism concerned, minor details of form and colour tended to be considered as merely stray brush marks of gene expression. This view still persists in some today who cannot bring themselves to accept my conviction that the patterns and colours on the wings of butterflies and moths have evolved as part of anti-predator defences.

In the 1990s, driving to my laboratory every morning, I went past billboards with the surrealistic tobacco advertisements that were ubiquitous at that time and found that I was taking time, while stopped at traffic lights, to try and interpret the messages. Why should there be an image of purple silk being cut with a knife? Why should there be a bird cage with a cigarette packet inside that became a bird in the shadow that was cast? Then I realised that many of these images had nothing to do with the product themselves but were puzzling me and grabbing my attention for many seconds while the associated brand name was being registered subliminally. Could it be, then, that when a foraging bird initially encounters a moth like the death's head it is confused in the same way we are confused by this kind of advertisement? Does it experience the same kind of assault on its perceptions that we tend to when viewing the paintings of Salvador Dalí or René Magritte?

A very few biologists thought, as I did, that there must be an explanation for the design of every feature, large or small, of an animal, however difficult it might be to prove this experimentally. The late Dame Miriam Rothschild FRS (1908–2005) was one of the most influential biologists to go *hors-piste* from the route to which the majority adhered. She proposed that features such as the yellow-and-black-barred abdomen and the mask of the death's head each served as an *aide-mémoire* to insectivorous birds, triggering fear of an encounter with hornets or giant bees.

I saw what Miriam was getting at when, in a talk to my local Village Society, I mistakenly showed a slide upside-down and suddenly saw the face of a giant hornet staring at me from the thorax of the death's head. It hadn't occurred to me up to that point that animals that forage for insects are more likely to see them head-to-head rather than obligingly orientated before them as in illustrations in an identification guide. After all, it is a central tenet of students of visual perception that faces are seen and recognised upright, and that affects our perception of most, if not all visual images.

Of course, there are many images you can see embedded on the wings of butterflies and moths if you care to look at the detail, eye-spots being a common example. But what, I wondered, might be the role of these disembodied images in survival when they are in the middle of a wing of a butterfly? I eventually got a clue to this from an unlikely source.

Thanks to Nikolaas Tinbergen (1907–88), the Oxford ethologist who shared a Nobel prize in 1973 for his work on animal senses and behaviour, we do have clear evidence that most birds and other animals have blinkered vision: they see details first in any object rather than the whole picture. It's as though if you went into a rose garden you would first see a rose and would not 'see' anything else – not the leaves, the lawns, hedge and layout of the beds, until you had identified that what you saw was a red rose and then built up the whole picture piece by piece. Some people will understand this immediately; the tendency to see detail first is common among people who are on the autistic spectrum and is also a feature of the affliction known as 'acquired prosopagnosia'[1]. The latter are generally incapable of face recognition because of failure to perceive the relationship between the various features. The psychiatrist and popular writer Oliver Sacks

---

[1] Literally, not recognising faces. A prosopon in Ancient Greece was the name given to an actor's mask, which represented his personality in the role he was playing.

(1933–2015) famously illustrated this with reference to a client of his who could identify his wife only by the hat she wore (Sacks, 1985).

Sometime later, I listened with increasing fascination to a talk given by Francis Gilbert (see Dietrich *et al.* 1993), one of the leading researchers in the field of insect mimicry. He and his colleagues had devised a simple test to learn more about the evolution of hoverflies, known to entomologists as syrphids. These are true flies with only one pair of wings, also known in the USA as 'flower flies' because of their habit of feeding on nectar. They are perfectly harmless – they neither sting nor bite, but everyone will have encountered a hoverfly at some time, most likely first as a child, and gone into an instant panic – many species are zebra striped in black and yellow or black and orange, as are wasps and hornets. It needs close inspection to see that they differ from wasps in having only one pair of wings. The second pair have been transformed into so-called 'halteres', tiny, club-shaped structures which are involved in the measurement of balance and flight speed. Apart from that, there is no sting, and the typical wasp waist is not there. But only a trained eye can spot these differences in the insect as it flies – or even when it is at rest.

The hoverflies are thus, to us, sheep in wolves' clothing. However, not all hoverflies – and there are very many species – are, to the human eye, good copies of wasps or hornets, and many seem to be very poor ones that look rather like houseflies. Are these at an intermediate stage in evolution? Or are they good enough copies to fool insectivorous birds? There is only one way to put this question to birds, and that is by experiment.

One way of testing the visual perception of animals is by the technique known as 'operant conditioning'. This was devised by the American psychobiologist Burrhus F. Skinner (1904–90), who used it to support his views that behaviour in animals and man is acquired, or 'reinforced' through processes of reward or punishment. ('Skinnerism' was famously satirised by the English writer and philosopher Aldous L. Huxley (1894–1963) in his book *Brave New World* (1932)). In seeking to identify the building bricks of the edifice that we know as the behaviour of a species, Skinner gave his name to an eponymous box in which an animal could receive, for example, a reward in the form of food if they made an appropriate response to a stimulus that was presented to them. Pigeons that were trained to peck at disks in order to receive a food reward proved to be ideal subjects for this study, becoming like obsessive gamblers. By training a pigeon to peck at a red disk, for example, it is possible to see by its rate of pecking whether it sees a disk of a slightly different colour – say pink – differently.

The question that Gilbert and his colleagues wanted to ask was whether pigeons would rank images of different hoverfly species along the same scale from fly-like to wasp-like as we humans tend to. To test this, they projected photographic images on to the transparent keys of a Skinner box. The surprising outcome was that the inter-mediates, half-way along the scale – the 'imperfect mimics' – were ranked by the pigeons as equivalent to the near-perfect mimics. This did not mean that the birds' discrimination was very poor, because they did show that they could detect what we would recognise as subtle differences between various degrees of 'near perfect'.

Is there a connection here, I wondered, between the incongruities in a tobacco advertisement and the presence of an unexpected wasp pattern on a harmless fly? This thought gave rise to a new hypothesis about a form of mimicry that depended upon ambiguity to confuse and distract potential predators. I decided to call this 'satyric mimi-cry' in reference to the mythical satyr that is half man and half goat. I published details of this concept with my colleague John A. Allen (1994), who knows more about experimental work on mimicry than I do, and it hit the scientific world like a damp squib, dismissed for lack of experimental evidence. A subsequent publication (2013), again in a peer-reviewed journal, drew the comment in the scien-tific press from a fellow biologist that I appeared to be suffering from *apophenia* – a tendency to see images that do not exist in reality.

Butterflies, Messages from Psyche was published in 2010. It contains many colour photographs of butterflies and moths that have embed-ded images on their wings, for example of snakes, toxic caterpillars, lizards, bird heads, fox faces etc. No doubt I let my imagination stray too far in a few cases. Nevertheless, the reviews were enthusiastic, but it became clear that some people could not see these images at all – perhaps even you who are reading this book will fall into this group – and I wanted to know why not. The winding road that I took in seeking answers to the riddle of the death's head hawk-moth shows that what we believe is reality is different for every one of us, and for all creatures, too.

1

THREAT AND SUPERSTITION

By some called Caput Mortuum, or Dead-Head, from the mark on the back, which much resembles a dead Scul, others call it the Jasmine Hawk, and by Mr. Ray, of Redland, the Pottatoe Hawk, but the Aurelian society chuse to distinguish it by the name of Bee-Tiger, but for what reason I know not.

Moses Harris (1731–85),
The Aurelian, 1766 (see Fig. 1)

Thomas Hardy (1840–1928), the great novelist and poet, is buried in the church at the Dorset hamlet of Stinsford near Dorchester – or at least his heart is. There was a compromise between the wishes of the State that he should be buried in Westminster Abbey, and his own wishes to be buried in the churchyard that figures in his novel *Under the Greenwood Tree* (1872) as 'Mellstock'. Some local people say that after his death his heart was delivered to his house in a paper parcel and was left on one side for a time, during which it was discovered by his hungry cat. The cat now, being a container for some of his remains, was buried there, too.

Many hundreds of people thread through the stone-pillared gates of the churchyard each year and head for Hardy's grave, shaded by yew trees and, as they do so, walk past a tombstone with a mysterious carving of a winged creature on the gravestone (Fig. 2). It has bat-like wings, and the eye is drawn towards a skull carved on the forepart of its body. The stonemason may have intended the image of a moth and, if so, this would almost certainly have been the death's head hawk-moth, a fearsome-looking creature that people sometimes mistake for a bat. Its name derives from the sinister pattern of a skull and crossbones on its thorax. It also has a broad, black-lined border to the underside of the forewings and to both surfaces of the hindwings, which appears to be marked on the sculpturing.

The death's head hawk-moth, *Acherontia atropos*, is the largest moth that occurs in Britain. It is also found throughout continental Europe and from southern Africa north to Finland. It rests with its brownish-black wings folded over its back leaving exposed the pale skull image, complete with what seem to be crossbones emblazoned across its thorax. When it opens its wings, it reveals vivid yellow underwings and an abdomen which is yellow, banded with blue-black satin bars (Fig. 6). Its image will be familiar to anyone who has seen the film *The Silence of the Lambs* or read the book on which the film is based.

No insect has had a closer association with premonition of death in European culture than this moth, a sentiment reflected in lines of John Keats (1795–1821): 'Nor let the beetle, nor the death-moth be/ Your mournful Psyche.' A skull, or an image of one, is a powerful symbol, variously signifying our mortality, impending death, danger or life beyond the grave. Why an apparent skull-and-crossbones image should be marked on the thorax of a large bat-like moth has always been an intractable mystery and this image still arouses superstitious fears today.

The Knights Templar, a religious and military Order originating among the eighteenth-century Crusaders, adopted the skull as a symbol of death and Satan, and gravestones of members of the order are found in Scotland with images of skulls carved on them. The skull was seen as a kind of coffin for the soul and was used in the indoctrination ritual of novices in which the knight, holding the skull, recited:

> May the spirit which once inhabited this skull rise up and testify against me, if ever I willfully violate my obligation of a Knight Templar.

The novice was then required to seal the oath with his lips seven times on the skull. Crossing the legs of a corpse on burial gave rise to the crossbone symbol, which was used as a sign of dedication to God, one which, incidentally, was also practiced in the tombs of the Egyptian Pharaohs as homage to the god Osiris. Freemasons took many of their mythological symbols and rituals from the Knights Templar and used the skull and crossbones as insignia of a Master Mason, but when it became generally known that Hitler's ruthless SS used the same insignia this practice ceased.

Carvings of skulls on gravestones also took place during the times of the great plague. The Black Death, which caused the death of roughly half the population of Britain in the fourteenth to seventeenth centuries, made its way into Europe from China along the silk roads and was finally brought across the Channel on a ship that docked in Weymouth Harbour (at Melcombe Regis) in 1348, only about eight miles from Stinsford. The *Grey Friars' Chronicle* records:

> In this year 1348 in Melcombe, in the county of Dorset, a little before the feast of St. John the Baptist [June 25th], two ships, one of them from Bristol came alongside. One of the sailors had brought with him from Gascony the seeds of the terrible pestilence and through him the men of that town of Melcombe were the first in England to be infected.

Within a month the disease had spread throughout Dorset to Devon and Somerset and had reached London by the following September. In the subsequent four years historians believe that more than 150,000 victims of the Black Death were buried in London alone. Altogether, about 75 million people and up to sixty per cent of the population of Europe are said to have died in the four-year global pandemic.

The practice subsequently developed of carving skulls onto gravestones of wealthy people. This was intended as a deterrent to grave robbers – a sign that the corpse was infected. It is believed that a skull was sometimes carved on a gravestone of someone who had died of other causes, rather, as nowadays, a dummy bell without a burglar alarm attached is put on to a house front.

The theory of defence against grave robbers may not completely resolve the mystery of the winged skull on Jane Knight's gravestone. She died in 1755, long after the plague had died out, but the practice of deterring robbers with the death symbol may have continued in some places. Although the cause of her death was not recorded, one alternative explanation may be that she was a victim of smallpox which was rife around Dorchester in the eighteenth century, as the following episode makes clear.

In 2009 Dorchester County Museum put on display a portrait, then just recovered from South Africa, of Benjamin Jesty (c. 1736–1816), a farmer from Yetminster in Dorset. It is claimed that Jesty was the first person to vaccinate against smallpox in 1774, anticipating Edward Jenner (1749–1823), an English doctor who is celebrated for that achievement, by 22 years. Jesty noticed that his milkmaids had never contracted smallpox, although they had been exposed to the virus, and he was aware of the common belief that people who had suffered from the far less virulent cowpox were immune to smallpox. He himself already had gained immunity from a previous smallpox infection and to test this introduced pus from an infected cow into the arms of his stoic and trusting wife and two sons with the result that they all survived the smallpox epidemic raging at that time. This immunisation made Jesty the target of ridicule from the local people; according to contemporary accounts, he was 'hooted at, reviled and pelted whenever he attended markets in the neighbourhood' and his neighbours taunted him with suggestions that his children would grow horns. In *The Return of the Native*, first published just over a hundred years later in 1878, Hardy also made several references to the previous smallpox epidemic: 'a disease whose prevalence at that period is a terror of which we at present can hardly form a perception.' It was in the same book, coincidentally, that he wrote about the death's head hawk-moth.

In recent centuries the moth has been commonly taken in folk mythology all over Europe to be an omen of impending disaster. Thomas Hardy (1878) made use of its sinister reputation in *The Return of the Native*. Wildeve, who is passionately in love with Eustacia, has the habit of announcing his presence to his lover by releasing a moth in her open window. The moth is then fatally attracted to the candle flame (as the doomed lovers are to each other) and is burnt to death as a result. Later, a game of dice between Wildeve and his rival is underway by the light of a candle. The game is interrupted first by ponies and then by a death's head moth that 'advanced from the obscure outer air, wheeled twice round the lantern, flew straight at the candle, and extinguished it by the force of the blow.' After this omen, the gamblers, undaunted and determined to continue, replace the light with a cache of thirteen glow-worms, adding to the undertones of superstition, and the desperate Wildeve proceeds to lose all his gold sovereigns.

In Bram Stoker's (1847–1912) *Dracula* (1897), flies and moths are among the 'mean things' that Dracula sends to Renfield, the inmate of a lunatic asylum who consumes them in order to obtain life force:

> Great big fat ones with steel and sapphire on their wings. And big moths, in the night, with skull and crossbones on their backs. Van Helsing, [the monster-hunter] nodded to him as he whispered to me unconsciously, 'The Acherontia Atropos of the Sphinges [sic] what you call the 'Death's-head Moth?'

Around the same time that Thomas Hardy was writing, the Rev. William Houghton (1828–95), a naturalist and clergyman, in his quaintly entitled *Sketches of British Insects – A Handbook for Beginners in the Study of Entomology* (1888), mentioned a superstitious belief that the death's head moth had been very common in Whitehall ever since the execution of Charles I. If that was so, the superstition must have persisted from 1649 when the king was beheaded – unless, of course, this was some entomologist's 'King Charles' Head'.

King George III (1738–1820) also appears to have had an encounter with the moth. The Cambridge Museum of Zoology has an exhibit of two death's head moths which were taken from one of his palaces. King George had five episodes of insanity during his lifetime. The moths came from Francis Willis (1718–1807) who became, assisted by his sons John and Robert Darling Willis, the King's physician during his third major attack in 1801. The King frequently asked to die as time went on and was greatly affected by the death of his daughter Amelia in 1810, age 27. One wonders whether the moths were preserved for posterity by Francis Willis because they were thought to have a special significance as an omen of death. The superstition around them was certainly known: there was also a conspiracy theory that the moths were placed in the king's bedroom for the purpose of provoking a fatal seizure.

One of the first depictions of the moth was by the Swiss artist Henry Fusili (1741–1825) who favoured supernatural images. In 1783 he painted *The Three Witches,* which included the three witches from Shakespeare's *Macbeth* (Fig. 3). They are gazing intently to the left of the picture past a death's head moth. This painting was later parodied to show three politicians gazing at the moon, which was an illusion to the insanity of King George.

In 1829, eight years before the beginning of Queen Victoria's reign, John L. Knapp (1767–1845), a clergyman, published a book which eventually attained wide popularity – *The Journal of a Naturalist* (1853) – in which he referred to the contents of a letter he had received from Poland:

> The dread excited in England by the appearance, noises, or increase of insects are petty apprehensions, when compared with the horror that the presence of this Acherontia [hawkmoth] occasions to some of the more fanciful and superstitious natives of northern Europe. In German Poland, where this insect is a common creature and so abounded in 1824 that my informant collected fifty of them in the potato fields of his village, where they call them the 'death's head phantom, wandering death-bird & c.' The markings on the back represent . . . the head of a perfect skeleton, with the limb bones crossed beneath; its cry becomes the voice of anguish, the moaning of a child, the signal of grief; it is regarded as ... the device of evil spirits – spirits enemies to man, conceived and fabricated in the dark; and the very shining of its eyes is thought to represent the fiery element whence it is supposed to have proceeded. Flying into their apartments in the evening, it at times extinguishes the light, foretelling war, pestilence, hunger, death, to man and beast.

The Victorian naturalist, the Rev. John G. Wood (1827–89), who was a prolific writer on natural history, noted in his *Illustrated Natural History* of 1863 that the death's head moth was regarded amongst the illiterate in Britain as some kind of extra-terrestrial messenger of pestilence and woe, or even a witch in disguise.

I once saw a whole congregation checked while coming out of church, and assembled in a wide and terrified circle around a poor Death's-head Moth . . . No one dared to approach the terrible being, until at last the village blacksmith took heart of grace, and with a long jump, leaped upon the moth and crushed it beneath his hobnailed feet.

Wood added, pompously, 'I keep the flattened insect in my cabinet, as an example of popular ignorance, and the destructive nature with which such ignorance is always accompanied.'

There was also a belief in the nineteenth century that the 'dust' from the wings of the death's head moth could render people blind if it got into their eyes. As we will see later, this moth has a loose coating of wax particles overlying the wing scales and a possible explanation for this belief derives from the possibility that these could float on the surface of the cornea, temporarily occluding vision.

In Germany the moth was used as a talisman in the late Middle Ages by farmers who nailed it to stable doors to keep away evil spirits. This is an echo of the ceramic eye amulets still used in the eastern Mediterranean area today to repel the evil eye, a symbol of which is also placed or painted on doors, boats, donkey carts and other forms of transport. In popular belief the principle behind using such amulets is that the evil eye, wherever it lurks, cannot tolerate its own reflection or likeness, so by analogy the moth's skull symbol, which also was seen as representing evil, would be a means of defending livestock against death and disease. In *The Golden Bough* (1890), Sir James G. Frazer (1854–1941), a Scottish social anthropologist and folklorist, gives many examples of charms used to protect cattle from wolves, witches and evil spirits, which included a pastoral crook, sometimes with mercury in the handle or a cross carved under a stable door and filled with salt.

The use of the moth in Germany to ward off evil spirits did not stop at pinioning the adult on farm doors. It was reported in 1757 by German naturalist and entomologist August J. Rösel von Rosenhof (1705–59) that the moth was so common in Halle (Händel's birthplace) at that time that farmers' wives brought baskets of the moths into the markets and sold them as amulets to drive away evil spirits.

These are most likely to have been the chrysalids turned up by the plough. The word used by von Rosenhof, *Alraunenmännchen*, means literally 'the little people of the mandrake root' (Fig. 4). The mandrake, a poisonous plant closely related to deadly nightshade, never seems to have been recorded in entomological publications as a food-plant of the death's head, although it might well be one. Magical powers were attributed to it in European folklore and its divided root was said to have a close resemblance to a small human figure. It seems that the mandrake had the same significance in mediaeval Germany as in Britain and Italy as a charm. In *A Modern Herbal* (1931), Maud Grieve (1858–1941) wrote:

> As an amulet, it was once placed on mantelpieces to avert misfortune and to bring prosperity and happiness to the house. Bryony roots were often cut into fancy shapes and passed off as Mandrake, being even trained to grow in moulds till they assumed the desired forms. In Henry VIII's time quaint little images made from Bryony roots, cut into the figure of a man, with grains of millet inserted into the face as eyes, fetched high prices. They were known as puppettes or mammettes, and were accredited with magical powers. Italian ladies were known to pay as much as thirty golden ducats for similar artificial Mandrakes.

The mandrake root in mythology was said to scream when it was pulled out of the ground. Coincidentally, the moth also squeaks when it is molested, so people may have seen a connection because of this. The dead moth with its wings closed also vaguely resembles a human figure. However, the chrysalis can also squeak and bears a certain curious resemblance to Palaeolithic Venus figurines.

According to the archaeologist Marija Gimbutas (1921–94) (2001), almost all archaeological sites in central Europe, the Balkans and Italy contain figurines at all levels going back to the Palaeolithic: 'We can often discern an artistic evolution from the earliest levels to the latest ones, indicating the importance of these objects to generation after generation of inhabitants.' Gimbutas estimated that the number of Old European figurines may be 100,000 or more. Doubtless many of these, which are about the same size as the moth chrysalis, were also turned up by the plough from Neolithic periods onwards. This points to the intriguing possibility that the artifacts and the hard-cased chrysalids were conflated in the Middle Ages and the symbolic significance of the former was shared with the chrysalids. Thus, the moth pupae and many of the artifacts may have served as amulets or devices to dispel evil, just as religious artifacts do to the present day. Paradoxically, then it appears that the adult moth may have been a symbol of death and a symbol used to oppose evil influences and, furthermore, that the pupa was a symbol of regeneration and also a talisman emptied to keep evil spirits at bay.

As the scientific revolution took hold in the Middle Ages in Western Europe, explanations of natural phenomena based on superstition were gradually jettisoned, and science and philosophy were in the hands of the few literate, the great majority of whom had been educated by clerics who challenged or ignored any explanation that conflicted with biblical teaching – as in the notorious case of Galileo. In 1633 he was tried by the Catholic Inquisition for expressing the belief that the sun was stationary at the centre of the universe and found 'vehemently suspect of heresy'.

In the field of natural history, however, science was largely confined to the cataloguing and description of species of plants and animals. In general, only members of the aristocracy with independent means were able to engage in 'natural philosophy'. One such was the French entomologist and writer René Antoine Ferchault de Réaumur (1683–1757), one of the greatest polymaths of the era. He gave his name to a temperature scale and made important contributions to mathematics, astronomy, the forging of iron and even attracted the interest of the Chinese with his proposal to farm spiders for silk (his treatise was actually translated into Manchu). He also is credited with writing the first text on taxidermy, stimulated by his interest in the physiology of birds. Regarded by some today as the father of ethology (the scientific study of animal behaviour), he published, from 1734 to 1742, six volumes forming the first comprehensive study of insects: *Mémoires pour servir á l'Histoire des Insectes*. In Volume IV he wrote a detailed description of the death's head hawk-moth and went to great lengths to find an explanation for the way in which it produced its strange high-pitched cries.

The people of Brittany, Réaumur noted, became alarmed in years in which they saw the moths, regarding them as harbingers of epidemic diseases and plagues. When he read an article by a Curé from Brittany written in 1730 in the *Mercure de France* in which it was said that 'the moth was cloaked in a manner that was the most sad that a funeral could offer, the wings marked like a kind of mortuary cloth', he railed against the superstition in *Memoires* Vol IV:

> Of all the countries in which it flies, Brittany is perhaps the only one in which one is told to fear it, where it projects consternation on the spirit of the people, and where it is looked upon as a herald of deadly diseases. The mind can act on the body in some circumstances; it can affect attitudes (dispositions), or at least augment those that affect illnesses, by which it strongly believes it may be attacked. But how does one free the people from prejudgement once received? It is transmitted from father to son… People read nothing at all…
>
> (Author's translation)

Despairingly, Réaumur went on to consider how one could educate the peasantry on the real causes of phenomena that frightened them. He took as an example the mysterious so-called 'rain of blood' in Aix-en-Provence and its surrounding neighourhood in July 1608. The common view, espoused by the Church, was that the 'rain' was the work of devils and of sorcerers. Here he took issue with the Church:

> Among the rains of blood that historians have reported to us as evil omens, there are among them those that are nothing more than red excrements which have been deposited by a large number of butterflies: only a supposed rain of blood at Aix and in its environs, towards the beginning of the month of July, and happily there was at Aix a philosopher, M. de Peirese, who proved demonstrably that this rain, which had been regarded as the work of the devil and of sorcerers, was due to butterflies.
>
> (Author's translation)

This 'rain', it appears, resulted from a synchronised mass emergence of thousands of butterflies, all of which released droplets of red-tinted gut contents (known as meconium), coming from the breakdown of the caterpillar tissues in metamorphosis that butterflies eject when they emerge from the chrysalis. Réaumur's opinion was that these droplets came from the large tortoiseshell butterfly, *Nymphalis polychloros*, which existed in France in that epoch in huge populations feeding on elms, sallow and willow, the adults usually emerging in early July.

Ockham's celebrated razor was widely preached at this time. William of Ockham (1285–1340) had reformulated a tenet articulated earlier, amongst others by Ptolemy (*c.* 90 AD–*c.* 168 AD) who said 'We consider it a good principle to explain the phenomena by the simplest hypothesis possible.' This conflicted with the view of the Church at that time, which was that nature was devised by God in this way to confound the peasantry. That appears to have infuriated Réaumur, and he was effectively adhering to this fundamental tenet of science when he insisted that the phenomena of insect metamorphosis were examples of God's supreme powers and artistry and not His devious roundabout way of punishing people.

Three hundred years later, essentially the same view of butterflies and moths (*Schmetterlinge* and *Nachtfalter* in German) was expressed in 1935 by Hermann Hesse (1877–1962). Commenting on a line from Goethe about the *Erstaunen* (amazement) that contemplation of nature evoked in him, he wrote:

> Whether I wonder at a moss, a crystal, a flower, a golden beetle or a cloudy sky, a sea with the evanescent giant breathing of its surf, a butterfly wing with the precision of its crystalline veins, the shape and coloured borders to its edges, the multiple language and ornamentation of its design and the infinite, sweet, magical subtle transitions and gradations of colours – every time that I experience with my eyes or with another bodily sense a piece of nature, when I am attracted and bewitched by it and open myself up for a moment for what it has to offer, then I have in that moment left and forgotten the whole avaricious, blind world of human needs, and instead of thinking or demanding, instead of competing or exploiting, of fighting or organising, I become in this moment nothing other than 'amazed' like Goethe, and with this amazement I become the

brother of not only Goethe and all other poets and philosophers, no – I am also the brother of all those by whom I am
bewitched and experience as the living world: of butterflies, of
beetles, of clouds, of rivers and mountains, for I am on the way
to amazement for a moment deserting the world of separate-
ness and entering into the world of oneness, where something
and Creation say to each other: Tat twam asi (This is you).

(Author's translation)

The Swedish botanist Carl Linnaeus (1707–79) originated the binomial system of Latin nomenclature of living organisms. He had a pro-
digious output. Part of Linnaeus's legacy, the naming of 14,000 plant
species, 3,198 insects, 1,564 shells, about 3,000 letters and 1,600 books,
is housed in the Linnaean Society library in London. The first edition
of his monumental work *Systema Naturae* was published as twelve
pages in 1735, but by 1758, in the tenth edition, it contained descriptions of 7,700 species of plants and 4,400 species of animals, among
them the death's head-moth, for which he chose the names *Sphinx
atropos*. Linnaeus would certainly have been aware of the sinister
reputation of the moth from contemporary accounts and from
Réaumur's writings (he refers to Réaumur for the use of the name *caput
mortuum* in his original description of the beast). This draws us again
into superstition and the mythology of Ancient Greece and Rome.

Mythology, especially that of ancient Greece and Rome, is not just
a collection of ripping yarns about supernatural beings but is a lexi-
con of icons with different characteristics. The Latin names of animals frequently established reference to fearsome mythical creatures.
The Sphinx was a predatory female ogre with a woman's face, large
wings and the body of a lion. She sat on a rock outside Thebes and
accosted passers-by with a riddle. Those who failed to answer it were
devoured[2]:

Her jaws dripped blood … as she sat on her high crag with outstretched wings, waiting to seize her prey and lashing her tail
like a lion, savage in her mouth, I asked her riddle. A terrible

---

[2] Seneca, *Oedipus Rex*

sound rang out from above and she snapped her jaws, tearing at the rocks. Impatient to tear out my living heart.

It was Oedipus who finally found the answer to the riddle, prompting the Sphinx's suicide. Oedipus then inherited the kingship of Thebes and the hand of Queen Jocasta, unbeknown to him as his father's widow. Nearly 2,000 years later his name was enshrined in psychiatric terminology by Sigmund Freud (1856–1939). The predicament of Oedipus then led to this dire warning from the satirist Tom Lehrer who urges people to be sweet and kind to their mothers:

Or you may find yourself with a quite complex, complex
And you may end up like Oedipus.
I'd rather marry a duck-billed platypus,
Than end up like old Oedipus Rex.

Before reading on, you may see connections between images of the Sphinx, the carving on the Stinsford gravestone and images of the death's head hawk moth, a subject I will consider further in the final chapter (Fig. 5).

Most entomologists favour a more prosaic explanation for the use of the name 'Sphinx'. Rather than the moth being attributed the generic name of a terrible monster, they believe it was inspired by the sphinx-like attitude of the caterpillar of this and other hawk-moths (see Chapter 2).

Acherontia is the generic name that is used today, later supplanted *Sphinx*. The name derives from the river Acheron that the souls of the dead had to cross to reach the gloomy sanctuary of Hades. The river Acheron flows from north-west Greece down to the Ionian Sea. It had on its banks the Necromanteion, a temple which housed an oracle where people came to hear from their dead relatives in Hades. In the north the river was regarded as the end of the upper world and the boundary with the underworld.

The species name *atropos* was the name of one of the three Fates, who were believed to control the length of life of an individual, thus making a further link with Hades, the vision of hell in Greek mythology. The three Fates were Clotho, who spun the cloth thread, Lachesis, who apportioned the length of the thread of life, and Atropos, the unavoidable one who cut the thread under the supervision of Zeus, who, it is said, sometimes intervened. John Milton (1608–74) in *Lycidas* refers to Atropos thus:

Comes the blind Fury with the abhorred shears
And slits the thin-spun life.

Lachesis is the specific name given to the sister species known as the greater death's head hawk-moth, which is found in the Oriental region and has recently become stablished in Hawaii. *A. styx,* the lesser death's head hawk-moth, which takes its specific name from the river separating the land of the living from that of the dead, is found in Southeast Asia (Fig. 9). Both moths have skull-like markings similar to that of *atropos.* Although the skull likeness is less convincing, the names nevertheless strengthen the association that these moths have with impending death. This imputation has continued until the present day, spectacularly fortified by Thomas Harris in his book and film of *The Silence of the Lambs* and persists in folklore, poetry and literature, as, for example, in the writing of the poet/naturalist Colin Simms:

The Death's Head, like to a queen bee's badge –
these moths go for hives, attack their honey
and even squeak like the proper residents
it's not only their death's head emblazon
though that had been enough in itself
but their translucent bright ghostly ribs

when one came into the little house at Boosbeck
my sister and I at the Duerr's jam it made for
thought a bird, a thought-bird, barged around
the walls and windows, curtains and light bulb
doilies and tablecloth and ginger beer jar

we were alarmed, excited, and wanted the insect
in our power, in our close sight to excite us
great grannie or whoever she was the moors woman
of Moorsholm declared it was for death, an omen

for death in the family. Myra died the next day
and the moth dead already under a tin tray
in the scullery, we preserved for our collection.

Colin Simms, *South Bank Poetry*
(with kind permission of the author)

In 2013, the moth had an impact on international cricket when it was deemed to have been an evil omen for the England cricket team in Bangladesh, who were playing the Netherlands – regarded as a minnow in the world of cricket. A death's head hawk-moth dropped into the commentary box to the consternation of the BBC commentator Jonathan Agnew. After an embarrassing defeat for the England team, Agnew later blamed the moth 'for the death of England cricket'.

Carl G. Jung (1875–1961) was skeptical of some aspects of science. He wrote:

> …there is created in the laboratory a situation which is artificially restricted to the question which compels Nature to give an unequivocal answer. The workings of Nature in her unrestricted wholeness are completely excluded. If we want to know what these workings are, we need a method of inquiry which imposes the fewest possible conditions, or if possible no conditions at all, and then leave Nature to answer out of her fullness.

In his method of psychotherapy, Jung found a way of using phenomena, such as the appearance of an omen, with a synchronous connected event. In his 1952 paper *Synchronicity, an Acausal Connecting Principle*, he introduced the idea that coincidental or synchronistic events were often part of the fabric of our spiritual existence and do not have physical causes, implying that such events represent the undetectable order in our lives which make them more than a series of random events. He got support for this concept from two Nobel laureates, Albert Einstein (1879–1955) and Wolfgang E. Pauli (1900–58), whose views were based on their knowledge of quantum mechanics. Pauli is famous for his 'Exclusion Principle', which helps to explain the interconnectedness of all the elementary particles in the universe (with then notable exception of the Higgs boson).

Jung found that individuals who understood the world only in terms of cause and effect were unresponsive to psychotherapy because, he said, such people always thought they knew better about the way the mind works. He (1960) quoted the case of a young woman patient with such rigid views that were melted away with the help of an insect:

> I had to confine myself to the hope that something unexpected and irrational would turn up, something that would burst the intellectual retort into which she had sealed herself. ... She had an impressive dream the night before, in which someone had given her a golden scarab – a costly piece of jewellery. While she was still telling me this dream, I heard something behind me gently tapping on the window. I turned round and saw that it was a fairly large flying insect that was knocking against the window-pane from outside in the obvious effort to get into the dark room. This seemed to me very strange. I opened the window immediately and caught the insect in the air as it flew in. It was a scarabaeid beetle, or common rose-chafer (*Cetonia aurata*), whose gold-green colour most nearly resembles that of a golden scarab. I handed the beetle to my patient with the words 'Here is your scarab.' This...broke the ice of her intellectual resistance. The treatment could now be continued with satisfactory results.

Synchronicity challenges our firmly engrained concepts of the universe and the nature of human existence. It is not accessible to statistical evaluation and scientific study – hence it is classified as paranormal. There will always be a vast majority of people who, like Freud, will regard the very idea of acausality as rubbish when explanations that appear simpler can be proposed, even though they are not all-embracing. But as one who has experienced this phenomenon many times, often as a vision in which there was great detail that did not relate to anything that was previously in my mind, and which each time presaged what ensued, I find it easy to accept that omens may occasionally in some people be symptomatic of synchronicity and therefore reinforce popular beliefs. Jung frequently referred to Lewis Carroll's (1832–98) Alice in *Through the Looking Glass* in which the White Queen discusses the advantage of living backwards:

'…one's memory works both ways.'
'I'm sure MINE only works one way,' Alice remarked. 'I can't remember things before they happen.'
'It's a poor sort of memory that only works backwards,' the Queen remarked.

2

THE SPHINX THAT DINES ON POTATOES AND HONEY

It is a mistake to think you can solve any major problems just with potatoes.

Douglas N. Adams (1952–2001)
Life, the Universe and Everything

Many people see the death's head moths not as evil omens or one of nature's fascinating curiosities but as nothing more than agricultural pests. The caterpillars can attack farm crops, and the adult moths can cause serious loss of honey production to beekeepers. As an illustration of this, we can take the so-called Sphinx caterpillar, *Acherontia styx*, the species of death's head that occurs in the Far East and attacks *Sesamum*. In Tamil Nadu it is controlled by deep ploughing to expose the pupae to birds, by hand-picking of caterpillars and two applications of two synthetic pesticides. The other cousin, *Acherontia lachesis*, is reported as a defoliator of teak in Malaysia. *Acherontia atropos* was a serious pest of potatoes before synthetic insecticides became available after the Second World War. To understand how this latter species became a pest, we have to look at the history of the potato and the biology of the caterpillar.

The Latin names of organisms frequently allude to fearsome mythical creatures, and because of these classical associations and because Latin was the *lingua franca* of scientists in much of the world in the eighteenth and nineteenth centuries, these names were easily assimilated. Most entomologists today believe that Linnaeus used the name 'Sphinx' for the death's head and other hawk-moths (which are classified in the family Sphingidae) in reference to the sphinx-like attitude of the caterpillar of these insects. When disturbed, the caterpillar lifts the front part of its body and bends the head downwards in a swan-like posture (Fig. 7) in the same attitude that a snake adopts, rearing up before striking. This is generally regarded by biologists as a defence against predators which the caterpillar can amplify by making clicking noises with its mandibles. The writer John R. Fowles (1926–2005) recalls his experience as a boy when he was given a caterpillar (1998):

> 'Oh the joys of that: the gloating countless times a day over its jam jar; the stroking that induced the poor thing to peep – a miracle, an insect that 'spoke'!
>
> All nature seemed human, its diverse forms puzzlingly near…cousins.'

As I noted, the generic name of the death's head was later changed from *Sphinx* to *Acherontia*. The species *atropos* that we know in Britain and Europe has never established a foothold in the New World. Its province extends from southern Africa and Madagascar to Finland from where it spread within the Arctic circle in 1996. Its crowning achievement in evolution, if you will excuse the teleology, has been the success of the caterpillar in conquering the challenge of feeding on plants, including deadly nightshade (coincidently named *Atropa belladonna*) and its relatives, which contain toxins such as atropine that are inimical to almost every other insect in existence.

Deadly nightshade, or Belladonna, is one of the most poisonous plants known. In Roman times, it is said that Livia used an infusion of the plant to lace fresh figs with which to poison her husband, the Emperor Augustus. Banquo, *Macbeth's* fellow lieutenant, is said to have presented to Harold the Dane, during the latter's invasion of Scotland, food supplies containing deadly nightshade which rendered the Danes hopelessly ill. The caterpillars of the death's head moth, however, are made of sterner stuff and are able to tolerate the poisonous alkaloids. They can even cope with cannabis, the highly toxic thorn apple (*Datura* spp.), which also contains atropine, and oleanders, *Nerium oleander*, which contain the powerful heart poisons known as cardiac glycosides; accomplishments which, except for the well-known example of monarch butterflies and their relatives which can tolerate the cardiac glycosides of milkweeds, are almost without parallel amongst insect species.

The death's head hawk-moth as a species had an amazing piece of good fortune in the sixteenth century. In 1565, the Spanish Conquistador Gonzalo Jimenez de Quesada (1509–1579) failed in his quest for gold but brought back to Spain instead a tuber that had already been a food source in the High Andes around Lake Titicaca for the previous seven to ten thousand years – the potato (Kiple & Ornelas, 2000). Over two hundred varieties of the wild potato have since been found in the Andean region of South America. The potato soon spread from Spain throughout Europe and was a valuable food resource in Germany during the late eighteenth century, mitigating the effects of famine caused by weather and military campaigns. The war of Bavarian Succession in the eighteenth century became known as the *Kartoffelkrieg* (potato war) because soldiers kept themselves alive by digging up potatoes until none of the tubers remained and the fighting then ceased.

Potatoes were first regarded with suspicion in Europe and Russia. They belong to the same family (Solanaceae) as the nightshades and contain poisonous alkaloids (which are fortunately destroyed by cooking) in the green parts of the tuber and in the leaves. Because of their shape, likened by superstitious peasants to leprosy nodules or even testicles, they were sometimes regarded as 'devil's fruit'.

In the years leading up to the French revolution, when there was starvation in France, King Louis XVI established a potato field in Paris in 1785 from which local farmers were eventually allowed to take plants. This kick-started the cultivation of potatoes on a wide scale. Marie Antoinette, his wife, who in her concern for the poor, allegedly expressed the hope '*Qu'ils mangent de la brioche*' is said to have worn potato flowers in her hair, a promotional stunt setting a fashion trend that was taken up at the time by other ladies of the Parisian aristocracy.

By the mid-nineteenth century, however, potatoes were accepted throughout France, after a period during which they were seen mainly as animal food. Jean-Francois Millet's (1814–75) famous painting *The Potato Planters* of 1861 was testament to their growing importance and Vincent Van Gogh's (1853–90) masterpiece *The Potato Eaters* (1885), showing a peasant family of five at the dinner table, made it clear that potatoes had by then become a main item of the diet of country folk rather than a last resort against famine.

Meanwhile, death's head caterpillars, munching away on the Old World poisonous plants for which they had acquired a catholic taste, found a new food available to them, conveniently planted *en masse;* a kind of vegetable burger from the Americas that was becoming more and more widely distributed and as readily available and plentiful to them as fast food is to us in the West today. Hence the caterpillar and the adult moth began to be recorded with growing frequency in entomological publications from the early nineteenth century onwards as potato cultivation grew (in 1846, sixty-three moths were officially recorded in England – undoubtedly a minuscule percentage of those actually existing then). That all changed with the spraying of chemical insecticides: first of all inorganic chemicals, including highly toxic arsenical compounds, and later organochlorines changed the picture completely and the *Acherontia* populations suffered the same catastrophic decline in Britain and Northern Europe as did, in their continent, ironically, the ancient Andean peoples that once used potatoes as their main food.

Nonetheless, in certain years, large numbers of moths have appeared – there were over 1000 records in Scandinavia in 1964 and 603 in England in 1956. It is believed that these moths bred in North Africa and Dalmatia, presumably feeding on wild Solanaceae, and migrated northwards, like the painted lady butterfly which breeds also in North Africa and underwent a huge migration northwards in 1964.

The ability of the death's head to feed on a variety of poisonous plants, including the potato, means that it can survive in relatively arid areas where many of these plants thrive – providing, that is, that honeybees are around to supply the adult moths with honey in an environment in which there is little soft fruit. The moths steal honey from beehives – *Acherontia styx* is notorious for this in Oman and *A. atropos* causes serious losses of honey at certain periods of the year in the Cape Verde Islands. The following extract from an article written for beekeepers by Ole Hertz illustrates the size of the problem (2001):

Death's head hawk moths present a seasonal problem for bee-keeping in Cape Verde. They are known in Cape Verde as Bambalutas. After the rainy season, which in Cape Verde means several days of showers in the autumn, bambalutas can be seen in great numbers. The bambalutas are attracted to the smell of honey and will wait around near the nests of bees and also try to enter hives.

If a large number of bambalutas get into a hive, the bees may be so disturbed that they will abscond. The bees will sting and kill some bambalutas, but their numbers can be so great that it is impossible for the bees to keep them out. The moths that are killed in the hive are embalmed in propolis by the bees and are found in large numbers inside the hive. Many moths get stuck in the hive entrance and sometimes it becomes completely blocked by the moths.

In the 'bambaluta period' a thick layer of dead, unpleasant smelling bambalutas are found in front of the hives with dust from their wings filling the air. The live bambalutas land in great numbers on beekeepers working with the bees. If you grab a bambaluta it produces a loud whistling sound.

Of course, conventional insecticides cannot be used around the hive to control the moths and special screens have to be attached to the hives to exclude them. It was the habit of stealing honey that earned the moth the alternative name of 'Bee Tiger' in the eighteenth century. How the moth manages to rob the honey without being attacked is another story which we will come to later.

3

THE ART OF COLLECTORS

Reading about the lives of the collectors, we sense that these are people who… have accidentally found the secret of happiness – concentrating with astonishing tenacity on the details of another parallel world – rising above the ills to which human flesh is heir, on the wings of the angelic butterfly.

Dame Miriam Rothschild (1908–2005),
Butterfly Cooing Like a Dove, Doubleday 1991

Up until the early nineteenth century, entomology was buoyed along by exploration. The discovery of new horizons, new species of plants and animals, and previously untapped sources of knowledge were great marvels for people of that era. Travellers returned from Southeast Asia with wonderful creatures, never before seen in the West: giant silk-moths, bird-wing butterflies and birds of paradise. From the African and New World tropics came blue morpho butterflies and moon moths of dazzling beauty, conjuring up visions of an earthly paradise. The exoticism of the tropical and subtropical world was brought to the popular imagination by the painter Henri Rousseau, whose inspiration came from visits to the Jardin des Plantes in Paris and from the stories of soldiers returning from the French expedition to Mexico. He is quoted as saying, 'When I go into the glass houses and I see the strange plants of exotic lands, it seems to me that I enter into a dream.' Such dreams inspired great works of art and, in turn, some of the poetry of Sylvia Plath and aspects of the popular children's *Madagascar* films.

The ancient Greeks believed that animals and plants had been put on earth by the gods for their benefit. Aristotle had divided animals into three groups according to their means of locomotion and their environment – walking, flying or swimming (land, air or water). Thus, whales and other marine mammals were considered to be fish, a practical classification that is apt for hunter-gather societies. It is also a means of dividing animals according to their most obvious characters: British naturalist Alfred Russel Wallace (1823–1913) noted (1853) that certain Amazonian Indian tribes considered hummingbirds and hummingbird hawk-moths to be one and the same to the point at which it was believed that one could transmute to the other at will, a belief that still persists here and there today.

Carl Linnaeus addressed the problem of defining the different kinds of animals with the publication of his *Systema Naturae* in 1737, adopting a two-part nomenclature reflecting the family and 'given' names common in most human cultures. Linnaeus's binomial classification of species was satirised by American writer and poet Herman Melville (1819–91) who, irked by Linnaeus divorcing whales from fish, proposed his own 'bibliographic' classification of Cetacea (whales, dolphins etc.) (2012). This was based primarily on size and secondarily on behaviour and habitat and separated these creatures into 'Books' (Folio Octavo and Duodecimo), each subdivided into separate 'Chapters'. This, he insisted, was pragmatic, as indeed it was to the hardened Nantucket harpooners risking their lives on whale boats in the nineteenth century.

Linnaeus, however, prevailed with his system of separating species by multiple anatomical features unrelated to size, means of locomotion or habits. By 1758, he had catalogued 4,162 species. The perception of nature changed radically: no longer were there different *kinds* of plants and animals in the world, representatives of which could all fit in to Noah's Ark, but there was a seemingly limitless number of creatures, each as different from the others as are books in a library all waiting to be catalogued. All Melville's 'chapters' had become subdivided into separate 'pages' each defined by often trivial details. In Linnaeus's scheme, the death's head hawk-moth gradually became three separable species as assiduous collecting in different parts of the world drew them to his attention: *styx, lachesis,* and *atropos.*

The age of the collectors had begun by the mid-nineteenth century and their fervour ensured that the number of recognised species had increased a hundred-fold by the end of the nineteenth century. Today, according to the *Encyclopedia Smithsonian,* insects comprise about seventy-five per cent of all world animal species. Conservative estimates suggest this figure as 1 million named species, but the total number including undescribed species may be 'between 2.5 and 10 million, perhaps around 5 million species' (Grimaldi & Engel, 2005). One Smithsonian Institute entomologist arrives at an estimate of 30 million living insect species (see www.si.edu/spotlight/buginfo/bugnos).

Natural historians in the eighteenth and nineteenth centuries became obsessed with collecting and naming (Pavord, 2004). In order to define insect species, taxonomists needed specimens that had been dried on setting boards with their wings (if they possessed them) spread fully horizontally, so that every detail of the upper- and undersides was exposed. Rows of set butterflies and moths in the glass-topped drawers of a cabinet made an attractive sight in which the wing patterns could be seen in resplendence. The combination of repeated colourful wing designs, the symmetry of the specimens and the way in which they were laid out has great aesthetic appeal and people began to flood into museums to lift the covers over the glass-topped display cases in order to see for themselves these beautiful creatures, and for the collectors, tapestries of coloured wings, effectively majestic works of art.

The setting and pinning of butterflies and moths in this way has had enormous consequences for the way we see them and relate to them. The dead insect is pinned through the thorax – that means through the 'skull' in the death's head moth – and the wings are then spread out horizontally on a setting board. All four wings and the antennae are pushed forwards with the hind edges of the forewings in a straight line and pinned under strips of paper so that they stay permanently in that position while *rigor mortis* sets in.

Visualise a butterfly or moth – the image that is most likely to come to your mind is one with the wings in a set position. This is especially so with the death's head moth because you may be familiar with the image on the poster and book cover of *The Silence of the Lambs*. More generally, we are bombarded with butterfly images in advertising, the vast majority of which show the insects again in this artificial set position, even when the message is concerned with the vitality that comes with the use of health products, perfumes, organic foods and so forth. If you reach for a guidebook to identify a butterfly or moth, the chances are you will find them portrayed also in the set position, which is a distorted image. It will have occurred to few people that lines joining the tips of the four wings with the insertions on the thorax form a cross in the set specimen: the creature which is seen as a symbol of natural beauty, vitality and grace on organic food containers and perfume bottles is in fact dead and crucified!

It is easy to compare insects when they were set and systematically arranged in a collection, and that led to the discovery of new species, a process that became addictive and offered the prospect of a mention in scientific publications and possibly fame to the discoverer and to the specialists who described them. Hence there were no limits to collecting, no quotas for collectors. Cabinets in museums and private collections were filled with numerous examples of every species obtainable. Over twenty specimens of the death's head moth will fill one drawer in a natural history museum, and there can be many such drawers (Fig. 10).

Whatever the underlying reasons, the desire to see a complete representative series of some object with all the possible variations is present to some extent in all of us, whether we are captivated by bird eggs, shells, postage stamps, bottle openers or insects. The collecting mania was fuelled by over-collecting, which hastened the extinction of species such as the large blue and the large copper butterflies in Britain. Like precious stones, they were prized because they were rare, and in the early part of the last century these insects could be found ultimately in hundreds in some private collectors' cabinets in Britain.

As collecting became more of a pastime, set specimens began to acquire commercial value, commensurate with their rarity and, as in postage stamps, aberrations especially so. The latter included unusual colour varieties of Lepidoptera, hybrids and gynandromorphs – specimens with mixed male and female characteristics. British nature writer Peter Marren[3] has documented the demise of the large copper butterfly, a species confined to marsh and fenland. This was attributed to a combination of drainage of the Norfolk fens, which were its main habitat, and collectors who were willing to pay farm labourers for the caterpillars or chrysalids. The insect became extinct in 1851, and by the end of that century scarcity of set specimens had led to dealers charging five guineas for one.

The highly prolific Victorian entomologist James W. Tutt (1858–1911) devoted about 47,000 words of his four-volume work on British Lepidoptera to the death's head moth, detailing every reported sighting, capture or observation and every visible detail and variation of the wings and body. Even a distant relative of mine who found a death's head moth in Yorkshire is documented. It was said that overwork brought on Tutt's premature death: it is difficult to believe he had time to sleep – but the same may be said of certain other entomologists in the late nineteenth and early twentieth centuries for whom understanding, rather than the devil, lay in the detail.

Huge numbers of butterfly and moth specimens have been lost; those that are not continuously curated soon perish, turned into dust by mites and museum beetles. The imagery of a death's head moth found in this condition was used symbolically in Susan Hill's prize-winning novel *I'm the King of the Castle* (1970). Death is a pervading theme and the young boy in the novel picks up a death's head moth from his grandfather's prized collection:

> He stretched out his hand, put his finger under the head of the pin and slid it up, out of the thick, striped body. At once the whole moth, already years dead, disintegrated, collapsing into a soft, formless heap of dark dust.

There was a sea change in the world of biology in the mid-nineteenth century brought about by the travels of Charles Darwin, Alfred Russel Wallace, Henry Walter Bates (1825–92) and Richard Spruce (1817–93), and the publication of Darwin's *Origin of Species* in 1859 (which had gone into a sixth edition by 1872). Wallace and Bates

---

[3] See Marren & Mabey (2010) for more details of this and other entertaining information about butterflies and moths

began as amateur collectors but dreamt of the naturalist's paradise they expected to find in the Amazonian tropical forest. Lacking the money and privileges that Darwin had, they funded their exploration by shipping specimens of butterflies, moths and birds to an agent in London who sold them to museums. On his voyage home after four years in the Amazon and on the Rio Negro, Wallace lost his collection in a fire onboard ship, only surviving himself after ten days in an open boat, but then took off again for eight years exploring, alone, Malaysia, Indonesia and some of the Pacific islands, encountering birds of paradise, bird-wing butterflies, flying frogs and the orang-utang. With far greater experience than Darwin had of tropical nature, he wrote, while pinioned by a bout of malaria, a comprehensive essay on evolution by natural selection which he sent to Darwin in manuscript. This was subsequently presented to the Linnean Society in London with a manuscript that Darwin had been working on for many years. After publication of *The Origin*, it was Darwin who achieved fame, ranking number twelve in *Time Magazine*'s list of the most significant people in history (seven above Einstein), and Wallace remains little known – even to many young students of biological science in Britain.

The Origin of Species, which every naturalist and biologist then turned to, was subtitled *Preservation of favoured races in the struggle for life*, and this book shifted the focus from cataloguing of species to searching for differences between related organisms that made it possible to define them as separate species. Taxonomists wished to know: 'When was variation within a designated species great enough to postulate sub-species?' 'Is this particular specimen far enough removed to be a new species?' Random collecting of specimens then became less important, less of a hobby, than collecting varieties, making it possible for taxonomists to search for clear differences between one species and the most closely related ones – divisions that often proved to be purely arbitrary. While the indefatigable Linnaeus had named the death's head *Sphinx atropos* in 1758, the generic name from thereon changed in the following sequence to: *Manduca, Acherontia, Brachyglossa, Atropos* and back to *Acherontia* again in 1877, and the specific name changed 21 times[4], each reclassification earning a taxonomist a place in entomological records. *Acherontia atropos* was

---

[4] ftp.funet.fi/index/Tree_of_life/insecta/lepidoptera/.../acherontia/

first used in 1910, but taxonomists looking at examples from different populations have named at least nineteen subspecies since then on the basis of characters that vary between different populations.

Meanwhile, Johann W. von Goethe's (1749–1832) thoughts about nature had been largely forgotten. Writing about a butterfly, he mused on the netted specimen, which lacked the most important aspect – life – which was the main part of its being and the key to understanding what a butterfly was. He restated this view in his most famous work *Faust* (1808):

Who'll know aught living and describe it well,
Seeks first the spirit to expel.
He then has the component parts in hand
But lacks, alas! the spirit's bond.'

Maybe William Blake (1757–1827) also had insect collectors in mind when he wrote his poem *Eternity*, published *c*.1793 (the lines of which are inscribed for more profound reasons on a stone plaque outside Exeter Cathedral).

He who binds to himself a joy
Does the winged life destroy;
But he who kisses the joy as it flies
Lives in eternity's sunrise.

When falling in love we may experience a 'fluttery' feeling in one's tummy caused by a reduction of blood flow to the organ. Germans call this 'Schmetterlinge im Bauch haben' (having butterflies in your tummy).

Now, if we are interested in understanding why a red admiral, a Camberwell beauty or a hawk-moth has distinctive patterns on its wings and why they are coloured so, there are two ways of looking at this. When the species concept was the focus of attention, most biologists accepted Darwin's conclusion that the evolution of bright colours was brought about by sexual selection involving usually female preference for the most colourful males, and that differences in colour patterns evolved to help to keep species apart by preventing interbreeding. However, this ignored the possibility that the colours and designs might help survival by protecting the insects. Bates, returning from his twelve years of collecting in the Amazon region with over three hundred new insect species, sowed the seed of a new theory which grew to dominate evolutionary biology. He wrote to Darwin with his conclusion that colours of many butterfly species from the Amazon region were used to advertise their distastefulness, and that there were many examples of edible species that had evidently evolved similar wing patterns, so gaining protection from predators. Bates's paper on this left Darwin, as Keats put it, 'like some watcher in the skies, when a new planet swims into his ken'. Darwin wrote to Bates in 1862 to say '...it is one of the most remarkable and admirable papers I have ever read in my life', adding '...it is too good to be largely appreciated by the mob of naturalists without souls...it will have lasting value.' Darwin's prophecy was correct. Bates's work generated an interest in mimicry that is still a main focus of the work of many evolutionary biologists today.

Until the middle of the twentieth century, studies on the evolution of mimicry in Lepidoptera were mainly based on the study of set insects. This bypassed the notion that selection would be proceeding through the action of predators that live in a different visual world from us and would see living butterflies and moths from different perspectives and in different attitudes and even possibly in different colours but hardly ever in the fixed artificial pose of set specimens. Understanding this furnishes the golden thread, enabling us to decipher the message of the 'skull and crossbones' of the death's head moth.

4

SKULLS AND ART

Bright contours inflame fear,
Yellow illumines black pain,
White outlines red, blood.
Wasp, hornet, tiger, vampire,
Wings black, dagger teeth,
Blenched skulls, hooked claws
Fiery eyes, porcelain-framed
Mementi mori – tokens of death

Lightning strikes dreaming nerves.
Fear ricochets in veins.
Life's slender thread quivers
Lachesis seeks her measure out
Atropos hesitates, hand poised-
Like a rearing cobra takes aim
Cold slivers of time pass
De pilo pendet – on a thread

(Author)

Skulls were used by the headhunters of Assam as trophies, a means of enslaving the soul of the previous owner for service in the afterlife and as guardians of tribal dwellings. Skull images have figured extensively in art as symbols of death. (Fig. 11) A famous mosaic tabletop from the ruins of Pompeii (79 AD) has a skull as the centrepiece. Poised over a butterfly, beggar's rags and a royal purple toga are on opposing arms of a balance broadcasting the message that whatever are the fortunes or misfortunes experienced in life they are nullified in death – an unforeseen irony for the people of Pompeii, who viewed the image of a skull as an exhortation to drink and be merry while they were able, anticipating the advice of Omar Khayyám (1048–1131) in his *Rubaiyat* (1859).

> Ah, my Beloved, fill the Cup that clears To-day of past Regrets and Fears – To-morrow? – Why To-morrow I may be Myself with Yesterday's Sev'n Thousand Years.

In the seventeenth century, after the Reformation, an art form developed in Holland in which the skull was again used to retail essentially the same message as the Pompeian mosaic – in essence 'whatever wealth and luxury you possess you cannot take it with you.' This was the *Vanitas* style, the name deriving from the Latin aphorism in Ecclesiastes 1:2: *Vanitas Vanitatis omnia Vanitas* (Vanity of vanities, all is vanity), 'vanity' here having the sense of futile hopes. Coincidently, this message is amplified in Matthew 6:19–20 with moths in mind, although St. Matthew was obviously thinking of clothes' moths:

> Lay not up for yourselves treasures upon earth, where moth and rust doth corrupt, and where thieves break through and steal. But lay up for yourselves treasures in heaven, where neither moth nor rust doth corrupt, and where thieves do not break through and steal.

Partly as a response to the ravages of the Black Death in the seventeenth century, many Dutch artists produced Vanitas paintings in which the transience of life was portrayed by symbolic objects. Sometimes these were insects, sometimes dead animals. A notable example is a painting in the National Gallery by Harmen Steenwijck (1612–56), painted in 1640, entitled *Still Life: An Allegory of the Vanities of Human Life*. Among the symbolic images he used were a tropical mollusc shell, books, musical instruments, silk, a Samurai sword and a stoneware jar. These objects represented the luxuries, pleasures and power that accrued to the lives of the privileged. They are set against the skull which dominates the picture as a representation of death and the threshold to a spiritual life, illuminated by a ray of light from above (i.e. the heavens). Although the message is religious in nature, suggesting that riches should be sought in heaven and not on earth, the irony is that the paintings themselves were acquired by wealthy people at great cost and became enduring financial assets.

Similar allegorical art continues to be produced in the present day and has been given new impetus by the British artist Damien Hirst. His diamond-encrusted skull *For the Love of God*, which is covered with 8601 diamonds valued at £14 million, was sold in 2007 for $100 million (approx. £50 million at that time). A mere print of this can now cost over £8,000. According to Hirst, the title of the 'sculpture' was inspired by his mother's reaction, 'For the love of God, what are you going to do next?' when it was first shown to her, but the fact remains again that the ostensible message that it is futile to accumulate wealth has made Hirst reputedly the richest artist alive. This irony has not escaped critics. According to a report in *The Guardian* newspaper[5]:

> In 2009, Spanish artist Eugenio Merino unveiled a piece entitled '4 The Love of Go(l)d', a giant sculpture, encased in glass, of Hirst shooting himself in the head. Merino, in fact an admirer of Hirst, intended the piece as a comment on the emphasis on money within the art world, and with Hirst in particular. 'I thought that, given that he thinks so much about money, his next work could be that he shot himself,' said Merino. 'Like that the value of his work would increase dramatically...Obviously, though, he would not be around to enjoy it.

It is nevertheless the artist Edvard Munch (1863–1944) who produced one of the most celebrated and powerful art works in history – and the most valuable (Fig. 12). The only one of four versions of his painting *The Scream* in private hands was sold in 2012 for 120 million US dollars. The figure in the painting, set against a dark background below a blood-red sky, has a ghostly white face which

---

[5] *The Guardian* headline: 'Suicide' sculpture of Damien Hirst causes controversy in Spain, 18th Feb. 2009

conveys an overwhelming sense of agony and horror. The face is thought to have been inspired by a mummy Munch saw in a museum and bears some resemblance to a skull. The figure in the painting stands against railings extending either side of it like wings and it needs little imagination to compare a death's head moth with this. Referring to one version of his painting, Munch wrote the following poem:

> I was walking along the road with two friends
> The Sun was setting – the Sky turned blood-red.
> And I felt a wave of Sadness – I paused
> tired to Death – Above the blue-black
> Fjord and City Blood and Flaming tongues hovered
>
> My friends walked on – I stayed
> behind – quaking with Angst – I
> felt the great Scream in Nature

The surrealist artist Salvador Dalí (1904–89) had an obsession with skulls as symbols of death. In 1934 he painted *Geological Destiny*, an empty plain with a donkey bearing two human skulls and in 1942 he produced two startling symbolic paintings, one of which was entitled *Soldier take warning*, for the campaign against venereal disease. Each was comprised of an illusory skull in which the cranium was a semi-spherical bell jar, the orbits were the heads of two women with combed dark hair and the teeth were the white flesh of the thighs exposed above their stocking-tops. Dalí was to develop further similar ambiguous skull paintings, but none led to greater interest than the one which made the death's head moth a movie star.

The death's head hawk-moth became the most famous insect in the world after Thomas Harris's book *The Silence of the Lambs* was published in 1988. In 1991, when the film was released, the moth was then propelled to stardom pictured on posters on the lips of the actress Jodie Foster. The film was an outstanding success. In the first four months of its release it achieved box office sales worldwide of $275 million. In 2011 this film was judged in an ABC Television programme as number one Suspense Thriller in nominations for 'The

Greatest Movies of Our Time'. An image of the death's head moth was the icon that was used to advertise the film.

The murderer in this book, Buffalo Bill, leaves a gruesome calling card in the throats of his victims: the pupa of a death's head moth – a symbol of death and metamorphosis. The fictitious entomologist from the Smithsonian Institution confirms the identification:

> The moth was wonderful and terrible to see, its large brown-black wings tented like a cloak, and on its wide furry back. The signature device that has struck fear in men for as long as men have come upon it suddenly in their happy gardens. The domed skull, a skull that is both skull and face, watching from its dark eyes, the cheekbones, the zygomatic arch traced exquisitely beside the eyes.

If, however, you are prepared to believe that the true *Acherontia atropos* figures in the book, the film and on the poster, then you will be mistaken on all three counts. Harris, who had researched his entomology meticulously in writing the book, makes it plain through his character Pilcher at the Smithsonian that the death's head moth in question was the Asian sister species, *Acherontia styx*, which was obtained from Malaysia, and not the European species.

Obtaining *Acherontias,* both pupae and adults, for scenes in the film, particularly specimens that were alive at the times they were needed for filming, posed a problem for the filmmakers. They got over this by using another large hawk-moth, the tobacco hornworm *Manduca sexta*. As the name suggests, this nicotine junkie is a pest of tobacco. Because it is easy to rear, as well as being an economic pest, it is a favourite laboratory animal for entomologists in the USA and can be reared continuously on artificial media, making it ideal as a stand-in for the real star. According to one report[6]:

> The Death's-head Hawkmoths that were first brought in got too cold and died immediately. The moth wranglers (Leanore G. Drogin, Raymond A. Mendez) had to order lookalike moths

---

[6] www.FreakingNews.com (website no longer active)

and put them in costume, made of painted fake nails cut into shapes and crazy-glued on. Unfortunately, the moths couldn't fly because the glue was too stiff, but eventually, a flexible glue was found. The moths were also attached with special string to sticks so they could be controlled and to make it look like the moths were flying.

When we come to the famous poster, the story is even more con-voluted[7]. Everything, except the skull, is *Acherontia atropos* (and therefore not *A. styx* as Harris decreed). Some commentators have described the skull as 'stylised'. This completely misses the point because it is not a stylised version of the moth you see but a moth with a miniaturised version of a painting by Salvador Dalí that is pasted onto it as a secondary image.

Two main themes stand out in much of Dalí's art: the female body and the skull, elements for him perhaps of the pleasure/pain dicho-tomy, but ones which he united in a living sculpture or *tableau vivant* composed of seven nude women in positions carefully choreographed to represent a skull. Dalí had used the image of a death's head moth in a reworking of a lithograph that was very popular in America: *The Life of a Fireman/ The Fire* (1854) by Nathaniel Currier (Fig. 13). He had decided to jazz up this picture to increase the emotional impact. In his version *Fire, Fire, Fire* (Fig. 14) he added larger flames and a death's head moth (representing a soul leaving the body) flying from one of the burning buildings. He also used the moth in his collabo-ration with the celebrated filmmaker Luis Buñuel in making the film *Un chien andalou* (An Andalusian Dog) in which the moth appears as a motif linking sex, death and sexual repression.

Dalí's novel conception of the living skull was motivated by his love of creating visual illusions, and the result was a painting entitled *Human Skull* consisting of seven women's naked bodies. Dalí began a collaboration in 1941 with the Latvian-American photographic artist Philippe Halsman (1906–79), who developed a considerable reputa-tion as a photographer; with Dalí he published a book in 1954 with 36 views of Dalí's trademark moustache. His other portraits include those of Albert Einstein, Marilyn Monroe, Richard Nixon, Winston

---

[7] For additional information see Howse, 2012

Churchill, Groucho Marx and Alfred Hitchcock, which are iconic in the literal as well as the figurative sense. Halsman assisted with the formation of the 'sculpture' – evidently a tough assignment that he and Dalí are said to have taken three hours to arrange. Halsman's photograph (1951), with Dalí alongside the naked assemblage, was entitled *In Voluptate Mors* (In Voluptuous Death) (Fig. 15) achieved greater fame than Dalí's original gauche sketch.

It is said that Halsman's photographic image was made available to the director of *The Silence of the Lambs*, Jonathan Demme (1944–2017), who then gave it to the agency DAZU (now defunct) to be used in the design of the artwork for the film. It is Dalí's painting of this *tableau vivant* that came to reside on the thorax of the moth which, with this transplant, was then placed against the lips of the trainee psychiatrist Starling (played by Jodie Foster) in the poster[8]. The symbolism of this image thus became very complex and provided a field day for art critics and amateur psychologists adept at deconstruction. Could the moth blocking the mouth of Jodie Foster represent repression of her feelings about death? Dalí's image incorporates a figure with outstretched arms – a possible reference to the crucifixion of Christ and therefore to reincarnation. Moths and butterflies in many cultures, it should be noted, are themselves believed to be souls of the dead, and insect metamorphosis is a common metaphor for death and rebirth.

It has been suggested by some that Demme's choice of image may have been in part a tribute to Buñuel and Dalí. In 2012, Dawn Baillie received the prestigious Saul Bass Award of Key Art (Hollywood) for her design work, with the following citation:

> Few modern posters have the eerie impact of Baillie's treatment of The Silence of the Lambs, where Jodie Foster's face is blanched into a creature with a trusting, helpless gaze and whose mouth is muted by a Death's-head hawkmoth. Despite the horrific nature of director Jonathan Demme's film, the poster succeeds not by amplifying terror but by potently evoking a psychological vulnerability that, like music, is hard to explain with words.

---

[8] www.highonfilms.com/the-silence-of-the-lambs-1991-the-voluptuous-death/

As an epilogue to this story, a portrait of Jodie Foster was published to mark the anniversary of the release of *The Silence of the Lambs*[9]. The fictitious Clarice Starling was traumatised by the silence that ensued when lambs were taken away for slaughter. A commemorative painting shows Clarice (Jodie Foster) smiling with a (saved) lamb in her arms and a death's head hawk-moth flying away from her.

---

[9] www.pajiba.com/.../mindhole-blowers-20-facts-about-the-silence-of-the-lambs-that-might-make-you-crave-a-nice-chianti.php

5

MONSTERS

The habit of seeing kings accompanied by guards, drums, officers and all those things which mechanically incline man to respect and terror, causes their countenance, when now and then seen alone, and without these accompaniments, to impress respect and terror on their subjects...

Blaise Pascal (1623–62), *Pensées*

Think of a fearsome monster – a dragon perhaps: it's not just a large reptile but an amalgam of features of potentially dangerous animals that combine to startle and confuse the senses. The combination of features that are never otherwise seen together in an animal is something unexpected, unknown and therefore frightening. The Chinese dragon, for example, typically has a camel's head, deer horns, hare's eyes, bull's ears, an iguana's neck, a frog's belly, scales of a carp, a tiger's paws, an eagle's claws and fiery breath. To an extent the death's head can be looked on as equivalent to a miniature dragon; as a result of the combination of its colour, body and wing design displays, sounds and odours that gives to the observer the impression of an alien creature, whilst to a potential predator, it remains an image that is essentially unclassifiable and confusing. There are a number of accounts in the literature to illustrate this.

The origin of the 'cry of anguish' that the death's head moth emits when molested has been regarded with superstitious awe in the past.

Louis Figuier (1819–94), a popular French writer on natural history, noted that this eerie cry can often terrorise a whole population (1875):

> In England, one hears it said this wild inhabitant of the air is in cahoots with sorcerers and that it goes and whispers in people's ears in its sad and plaintive voice, the name of the person that death will soon carry away.

Figuier rejected this interpretation but seemed to agree that the moth is an alien, part of Nature's scheme for filling all hours of the day by making available contact with divine sources with glimpses of another world. 'What a happy mission for science and for the heart of a naturalist,' he added, 'to be able to dispel one of the thousands of prejudices of the superstitious and ignorant.'

While the role of the 'voice' remained a mystery, naturalists concentrated on the puzzle of how it is produced. Réaumur in 1742 began with the assumption that the proboscis had a role in this. The proboscis in the death's head is unusually short, for reasons that will emerge later, and can be projected out between two short mouthpart appendages known as palps. Réaumur thought the tough proboscis rubbed against ridges on the palps to produce the squeak. He then cut off one of the palps, after which the sound was barely audible. When he severed the proboscis, the moth remained mute.

Although this seemed to settle the matter, controversy raged for another two centuries. Some entomologists were Réaumur supporters, others believed different joints in the body were involved. Then there was the theory that the proboscis was acting like a flute and another that the sound arose from air being blown out of the spiracles (breathing holes), and yet another that it came from air being blown over a pair of hair fans on the abdomen. Around 1840, several naturalists drew attention to these fans of hairs that were deployed each side from cavities in the second segment of the abdomen of the male moths when they were held in the hand. This was accompanied by sounds. It was claimed that the individuals without these fans (the females) had no voice, and so the answer to the conundrum seemed obvious. Eventually, the way in which the moth produces sound was explained in 1872 by Henry N. Moseley (1844–91) who took an experimental approach:

I was killing a specimen…by means of a solution of cyanide of potassium, which I was using with a pen in the ordinary manner, the animal squeaking loudly under the operation. A drop of the fluid happened to fall on the extremity of the proboscis. I noticed that at each squeak a large bubble was formed, showing a forcible expiration from the organ. I repeated this experiment constantly with water, and always with the same result. I further extended the trunk with a pin during the emission of the sound, and noticed a modification in the tone of the cry, which varied with the amount of extension. These experiments convinced me that the sound came from the proboscis, and was produced by an expiration.

It is not then surprising to learn that after a moth has been feeding on honey it is unable to squeak!

Moseley found a cavity at the base of the proboscis which could be compressed by muscles, thereby forming a bellows to drive air through the proboscis – a unique invention among insects: nature's equivalent of an organ pipe. Over eighty years later, in 1959, two French biologists, Busnel and Dumortier, showed that the squeak is produced in two parts: by sucking air in while vibrating a membrane at the entrance to the pharynx to produce a trill of rapid clicks and then forcing the air out to produce a sustained tone like that produced by a flute or the drone of bagpipes. The main frequency of the first part is around 6 kilohertz (kHz) (two to three octaves above middle C), while that of the second is about 10 kHz with higher harmonics (20, 30, 40 kHz) in the ultrasound range.

The general view among biologists today is that the squeak is part of the moth's defences. It is often described as 'squeaking like a mouse' and runs around looking like one, with the white spots on its blackish forewings resembling eyes and amplifying the illusion. This may be enough to confuse insectivorous birds. Interestingly, the sound is similar to the rapid clicks produced by hibernating peacock butterflies when they are disturbed by rodents. The sounds seem 'mournful' because the clicks undergo a downward sweep in pitch, a bit like music changing from a major to a minor key. Curiously, the ultrasonic echolocation calls of some bats do the same, but this serves to make it easier for a bat to compare the broadcast sound with the echo. There remains a possibility then that the moth's cry, particularly its high harmonics, may be used to confuse insect-feeding bats[10]. The hearing of rats and mice extends from about 0.25 kHz (around middle C) right into the ultrasonic hearing range up to about 100 kHz. The average person hears little above about 13–14 kHz, so what sounds barely audible to us can, at close range, be potentially deafening to rats and mice.

> Wee, sleekit, cowran, tim'rous beastie
> O, what a panic's in thy breastie
> Thou need na start awa sae hasty
> Frightened by a squeaking moth
> It wad be laith to rin an' chase thee
> It's only bluff to put thee off!
> (Author, with apologies to Robert Burns)

Certainly the 'hair fans' or 'hair pencils' as they are generally known today were displayed at the same time as the moth's 'voice' was heard, but that is as far as it went. One view was that the folded hairs were nothing to do with sound production but were used to tickle the female genitalia in a kind of moth fellatio. The fans were described by Archibald H. Swinton (1812–1890) in 1880 thus:

> …when the male…is on the point of squeaking in our fingers, as its abdomen inflates, a sessile pencil of yellow hair starts from a fold…expanding to a stellate form with swift whirling motion, like a trundled mop…and immediately there arises an oily volatile effluvia, resembling the scent of jessamines [jasmine], but soon becoming nauseous. This fluid aroma, secreted near the insertion of the 'fans', and traversing by capillary action to their extremity, stains them bright orange…shading to yellow at their tip.

Bringing the scent brushes into the argument was, however, a distraction. They are used by the males of many moth species (and some butterflies) as a prelude to courtship. In the human species, in contrast, it

---

[10] See also Chapter 6

is generally the ladies that are encouraged by advertisers to use scents as an aid to seduction. In some older forms of Morris dancing, on the other hand, men moistened their handkerchiefs under their armpits, where the perspiration contains compounds related to testosterone, and waved these in front of women – an element of courtship that cultural values have eliminated today. There is, however, no unequivocal evidence that synthetic perfumes marketed for men enhance their sexual allure.

The moth scent has been identified by Dutch scientists and contains a mixture of terpenoids – chemical substances that can be found in many herbaceous plants and pine oils to which they impart pleasant scents – but strangely they are all synthesised *de novo* by the moth in spite of the fact that many are contained in the food plants (e.g. jasmine) of the caterpillars. Nature is usually more parsimonious.

Despite the superficial resemblance of the squeak to the 'piping' sound made by queen honeybees that has been shown to calm workers in the hive, there is no evidence that it serves a similar purpose when the moths raid beehives. For biologists the sound is a 'disturbance sound' and the odour a 'repellent'. Now try and imagine what this means to a moth. The death's head moth is about the same size as a mouse, so a mouse encountering the moth at close range might perceive the equivalent of what a dragon is for us: a huge creature with the black and yellow legs of a tarantula spider, the black and yellow body stripes of a tiger, whilst meanwhile producing a noise as loud as a pneumatic drill sounds to us. The sound, probably deafening to the mouse, is accompanied by the sudden appearance of whirling structures resembling bright orange toilet-cleaning brushes each the size of the moth's head, and by a powerful odour of disinfectant mixed with rancid fat.

Ben Okri's description (2007) of a masquerade – a Nigerian spirit ancestor entering the physical world – conjures up dread that perhaps helps us to appreciate the shock a mouse might feel from similar sensory overload:

It shone and blazed in rich colours of red and yellows, with black toes, white feet, purple legs, and glittering, flaming materials of orange and gold, of red and violet and green…with its enormous presence, its branches of fire and flashing lightening, black smoke billowing from its vents, was like the figure of a terrible deity.

Edgar Allen Poe (1809–49), the writer and poet who was obsessed with death and omens of disaster, gives a view from another perspective when writing about a vision he had while visiting New York during a time of cholera. In his short story *The Sphinx* (1846) he described a gigantic and horrible winged apparition on the side of a hill, which, from his perspective, was the size of an ocean liner and equipped with a proboscis sixty or seventy feet long.

…there were outspread two pairs of wings – each wing nearly one hundred yards in length – one pair being placed above the other, and all thickly covered with metal scales; each scale apparently some ten or twelve feet in diameter. …the chief peculiarity of this horrible thing was the representation of a Death's Head,…While I regarded the terrific animal, and more especially the appearance on its breast, with a feeling of horror and awe – with a sentiment of forthcoming evil, which I found it impossible to quell by any effort of the reason, I perceived the huge jaws at the extremity of the proboscis suddenly expand themselves, and from them there proceeded a sound so loud and so expressive of woe, that it struck upon my nerves like a knell and as the monster disappeared at the foot of the hill, I fell at once, fainting, to the floor.

Poe lived all his life in America and is unlikely ever to have seen a death's head moth, but his host in the story interprets his vision while looking at the moth from where the terrified writer was sitting and finding the phantasmagorical object to be a tiny fly only a sixteenth of an inch long and a sixteenth of an inch away from his pupil, thus giving us two lessons in one about the vagaries of human perception.

This book, however, is not just about how WE perceive the world, or more specifically a weird moth, but how animals perceive it. To try and understand this I will focus first on honeybees, whose world is largely defined by odours, and then on bats and birds where hearing and vision are the dominant senses.

FIGURE 1: Bee-Tiger (showing the caterpillar, pupa and adult) *The Aurelian*, 1766, Plate 37, by Moses Harris (1731–85).

FIGURE 2: A tombstone in St. Michael's Church, Stinsford, Dorset, 'Here lies the bod [sic] of Jane wife of John Knight who departed this life May 17th, 1755 aged 80.'

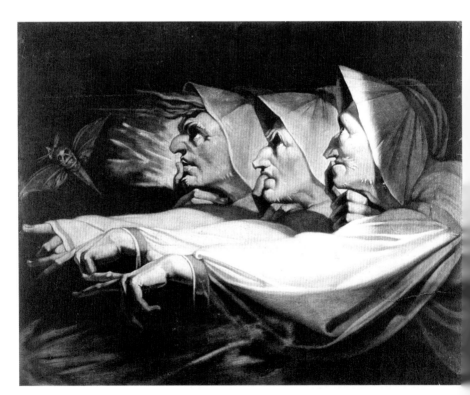

FIGURE 3: The Three Witches in Shakespeare's *Macbeth* (showing a death's head hawk-moth on the left), Mezzotint by J.R. Smith, 1785, after Henry Fuseli, 1783. Wellcome Foundation Museum Public domain, via Wikimedia Commons.

FIGURE 4: Mandrake (*Mandragora officinarum*) with a dog, from the *Tacuinum Sanitatis* manuscript (*ca.* 1390). Dogs were used to pull the root out of the ground to avoid its mystical properties harming their owners. Unknown author, public domain via Wikimedia Commons.

FIGURE 5: Sphinx statue guarding a fountain (Osborne House, Isle of Wight).

FIGURE 6: The mysterious 'skull and crossbones' sign on the thorax of the death's head hawk-moth seemingly supported on the yellow pedestal of the abdomen.

FIGURE 7: Caterpillar of the death's head hawk-moth in its 'sphinx' posture, also resembling an open-mouthed snake. Note the false head at the end of the body and the stripes that disrupt the visual outline of the body.

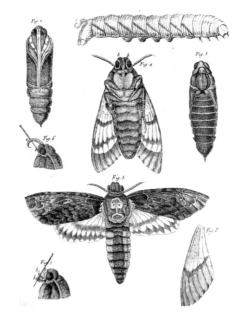

FIGURE 8: Illustrations of the death's head hawk-moth, its pupa and caterpillar from Réaumur's *Mémoires pour servir à l'Histoire des Insectes* (1744). The unusually short proboscis, adapted for feeding from the honeycomb, is figured on the left of the plate.

FIGURE 9: Icons of the Fates and of the River Styx (top down): *Acherontia lachesis, A. styx* and *A. atropos* (Courtesy of Jean Haxaire).

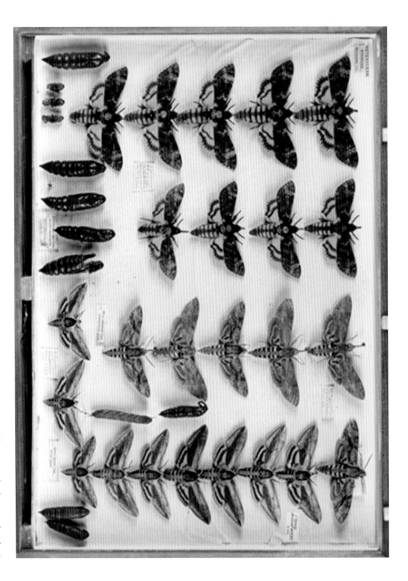

FIGURE 10: A late Victorian hawk moth collection: death's head hawk-moths alongside convolvulus and privet hawks in the cabinet of the Rev. Arthur Miles Moss (Courtesy of Kendal Museum).

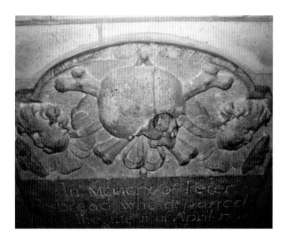

FIGURE 11: Skull and crossbones on an eighteenth-century tombstone possibly of a crusader at St Mary's Church, Portchester Castle, Hampshire.

FIGURE 12: *The Scream* by Edvard Munch. With permission from Munch Museum, Norway.

FIGURE 13: *The Life of a Fireman/The Fire* by Nathaniel Currier; Michele and Donald D'Amour Museum of Fine Arts, Springfield, Massachusetts; Gift of Lenore B. and Sidney A. Alpert, supplemented with Museum Acquisition Funds; photograph by David Stansbury.

FIGURE 14: *Fire, Fire, Fire* by Salvador Dalí; Michele and Donald D'Amour Museum of Fine Arts, Springfield, Massachusetts; Gift of Lenore B. and Sidney A. Alpert, supplemented with Museum Acquisition Funds; photograph by David Stansbury.

FIGURE 15: The *tableau vivant 'In Voluptate Mors'* arranged by Salvador Dalí and photographed by Philippe Halsman © Philippe Halsman/Magnum Photos.

FIGURE 16: Attic vase from around 540 BC at the British Museum (with permission) showing four figures taking honey from hives meant for the infant Zeus. They try to defend themselves against the attack of the bees.

FIGURE 17: Death's head moth feeding unmolested on a honeybee comb. (Photo © Y. & J.-L. Pelouard)

FIGURE 18: Bird's eye view of the skull mark on *Acherontia atropos*. Features such as compound eyes, simple eyes, antennae (each side of the head), jaws, and a yellow and black-striped abdomen can be made out, which resemble the head of large, hornets or wasps with black-striped yellow and orange warning colours, e.g. Asian giant hornet and/or Mammoth wasp (see Figs. 19 & 20 below)

FIGURE 19: The head of an Asian giant hornet, *Vespa mandarinia japonica* (Photo © Yasunori Koide, Wikimedia Commons).

FIGURE 20: Mammoth wasp, *Megascolia maculata* – another possible model for mimicry by the death's head hawk-moth. (Photo © Mike Sway NoDerivs 2.0 Generic (CC BY-ND 2.0) Wikimedia Commons).

FIGURE 21: The 'sparrow' image on the wings of the death's head hawk-moth. Fledgling birds may see such an image of their parents while they are in the nest. The orange spots may represent the eyes and beak, the white spots nostrils. The wing markings suggest the wings of the bird drawn forward over the head. The pale lines at the wing tips suggest claws.

FIGURE 22: The death's head hawk moth (left) showing its defensive posture in which colour bands on the forelegs are exposed and the yellow-tufted appendages below the mouth, part of its 'ears', are flipped forwards as part of the display. Right: For comparison, a lycosid wolf spider in defence mode. Photo © Frank Buchler (www .virtualartifex.com).

FIGURE 23: *Acherontia lachesis*, the greater death's head hawk-moth; Java (actual size of insect). Photo © Thomas Schoch (www.retas.de) CC BY-SA 3.0

FIGURE 24: Roman head joined to a more recent torso of statue with a Medusa breastplate, Ashmolean Museum, Oxford.

FIGURE 25: Caravaggio's painting of the severed head of the Medusa, Uffizi Gallery, Florence. Public domain via Wikipedia Commons.

FIGURE 26: Athenian 'black figure' drinking bowl, fifth century BC (Ashmolean Museum, Oxford) **Above**: Head of the Gorgon Medusa is portrayed in the centre on a ceramic bowl, with surrounding figures enjoying a symposium beneath vines. Some figures hold drinking vessels and there are musical instruments shown, i.e. an aulos and a lyre. **Below**: Reverse side of the Medusa drinking bowl. Inverting the page shows the eyes and penis symbols more clearly.

FIGURE 27: Stone carving of the Gorgon Medusa from the Temple of Artemis, Corfu (580 BC). The demonic features are believed to have served to prevent evil spirits from entering the temple.

FIGURE 28: Mosaic of Alexander the Great from the House of the Faun, Pompeii, showing the Medusa head on his breast-plate. Unknown author, public domain via Wikimedia Commons.

6

THE HONEYBEES' TALE

I know that if odour were visible as colour is, I'd see
the summer garden aureoled in rainbow clouds,
with such warfare of hues as a painter might choose
to show his sunset sky or a forest aflame;
while o'er the country-side the wide clover-pastures
and the beanfields of June would wear a mantle, thick
as when in late October, at the drooping of day
the dark grey mist arising blotteth out the land
with ghostly shroud.

Robert Bridges (1844–1930) *The Testament of Beauty*

Animals of all kinds live in a quite different sea of sensory impressions from us. In many, smell is the dominant sense, and the behaviour of many species is dictated by the perception of odours to which we are oblivious, and scent fields of the kind that the poet Robert Bridges imagined. But the terms 'environment' and 'world' are only crude descriptions of the space around us which we can sense and which we have explored for ourselves rather than imagined. The German word *Umwelt*, used by the pioneer German ethologists, is more useful here: it means literally the 'surrounding world' and stands for the part of the environment that animals (or people) inhabit and experience. I will translate this as the 'near-world', and this for honeybees is one in which their 'reality' is constructed mainly from odours, and it is odours that are the bosons of the societal cosmos, knitting individual bees together in an interconnected group that functions like a superorganism.

Our understanding of insect societies owes a great deal to the late Bill Hamilton (1936–2000), an evolutionary biologist known to few outside the biological sciences. His work led to the founding of the science of Sociobiology, and he is regarded as the leader of what has been called the second Darwinian revolution. A quiet man, soft spoken and introspective, he was unpopular with undergraduates because he would wander off the topic during lectures on evolutionary genetics and start developing on the blackboard some idea that had just occurred to him as he was speaking. Not what the syllabus-bound undergraduate of latter years appreciates but more, perhaps, in the tradition of the Greek philosophers. His insight into the genetics of inheritance explained the forces that led bees, wasps, ants and termites to live in societies. His obsession with social insects led to him getting badly stung by social wasps on an expedition to the Mato Grosso in Brazil, and his swollen face was recorded for posterity in the book of the Royal Society and Royal Geographical Society expedition in 1967–69 (Smith, 1971). Sadly, it was actually a very unsocial insect – a mosquito – that was responsible for his premature death from malaria in 2000, contracted during a research visit to Central Africa to study tropical diseases.

Honeybee workers, like those of all truly social insects, will cooperate in finding food and defending each other and the queen, often giving up their lives to do so. When a honeybee stings, the sting shaft is torn from its body along with the poison sac, as a result of which the bee will die. Martyrdom without a cause it might appear to be, because worker bees are sterile females (with undeveloped ovaries), and therefore it appears at first sight that there is no benefit gained from this altruism because none of the workers that survive can pass on their genes.

Hamilton saw the answer to this conundrum, simple but obvious once conceived, like all great insights. The workers in the hive are sterile but are all daughters of the queen and share most of her genes, so that if the workers help the queen to produce more queens at the end of the season that leave and found new colonies, those same genes tend to persist from generation to generation. The queen bee inhibits the development of ovaries in the workers (female offspring) by means of the 'queen pheromone' she secretes, which is like an externally acting hormone, so they do not all start rearing their own brood which would lead to breakdown of the society.

If survival with the best set of genes is the wind that fills the sails of the limitless fleet of evolving organisms, then the fabric of the sails in honeybees is made of odours: flower scents, bee odours, volatile chemicals. Scent plays little part in our daily lives. In fact, there are numerous commercial products like deodorants, air fresheners, etc. that are designed to suppress our sense of smell, and many perfumes that mask body odours completely, substituting scent notes that we find pleasing. In contrast, dogs are known to have a sensitivity to smells which is about 1000 x greater than ours. They are well known for their ability to detect substances that are sometimes odourless to us, given off, for example, by hidden drugs, explosives, cancerous tumours, buried bodies, etc. Bees can also detect infinitesimally small amounts of organic chemicals (especially flower scents and pheromones) in their environment and can even be trained, like dogs, to detect the presence of landmines by the vapour given off by explosive materials, even though the concentration in air may be in parts per trillion. The following, which is part of a report from researchers at the US Air Force Research Institute (AFRI) and the University of Montana (Bromenshenk *et al.*, 2003), while explaining the fascinating results of an empirical study with great scientific exactitude, reveals little of how scientists picture and evaluate the world, each word having a precise meaning that conjures up images to which the layman has no key:

…we observed that bees behaved like a very fine-tuned, nearly ideal detector at vapor levels higher than 10 pptr from 2.4-dinitrotoulene (2.4-DNT) mixed in sand. In 2001, AFRL and we calculated a detection probability of 97–99 percent at parts per billion (ppb) and parts per trillion (pptr) vapor concentrations, with a 1.0–2.5 percent probability of false positive and less than one percent probability of false negative. In the 2002 tests, bees consistently detected DNT targets generating 50–80 pptr vapor. Under moist conditions, this dropped to about 30 pptr. AFRL predicted that with sufficient numbers of bees, the detection threshold could go even lower.

On reading this, you will perhaps understand how difficult it is for a scientist (and I include myself in this) to descend (or ascend) the spiral staircase from the gallery of his or her original unique coded pictures of reality and explain them to those on another level who may reach out to reality through art, poetry, literature and music.

Although we would be able to smell many odours that a dog can, were they in high enough concentration, there are many that we cannot detect at all. It is commonly said that we have lost much of our sense of smell because it is not relevant to us in the modern world. Certainly, our sense of smell diminishes as we age and fluctuates according to moods and interest in sex, for example, but anthropologists and ethnologists have discovered striking cultural differences in the role of smell in communication.

In the western world, sight and sound are dominant to smell, presumably because our anthropoid ancestors needed to be instantly aware of threats from enemies and predators. Victorian, scented gardens have been replaced by those with plants chosen on the basis of their colours. Varieties of tomatoes and carrots grown for mass consumption have lost the taste and scents of older varieties, features that have been lost because of preference for shape, size, and colour. We tend to choose what we eat from pictures of food in cookery books, magazines and television screens, independently of texture, smell, taste, temperature, etc. In contrast, in certain Amazonian tribes the choice of food, particularly of the type of meat, is based on smell. The Canadian anthropologist David Howes, writing about the baskets woven by the Tukano people of the Amazon (in Classen *et al.*, 1994), notes that we in the Western World looking at these in a modern museum have only a limited perception of the exhibit:

> Appreciating the visual design of a Tukano basket would tell one nothing of the range of sensory characteristics which are meaningful to the Tukano, right down to the odour of the vines from which a basket is made.

Helen, a former research student of mine, went into the Amazonian forest in Brazil with a group of others but wandered off on her own and got lost. This is very easily done, and the best thing is then to light a fire, if you have the means, to signal your whereabouts.

Although she was not able to do that, she was fortunately located after about two hours. She was told that the ultimate resort would have been for the searchers to recruit the local Caboclos (detribalised Indians) who would have found her by smell from up to a mile or so.

Remarkable as it may seem, this ability to detect odours to which we in our towns and cities are insensitive is highly developed in some of the Amazonian tribes that have been studied. The Desana people of Colombian Amazonia discriminate between members of different tribes on the basis of how they smell. The specific odours are related to factors, including what they eat, and the odours of plants and animals in their near-world. While walking through the forest, they constantly sniff to see whether people of other tribes have been present[11]. The Desana also distinguish between different individuals by their smell, which is a combination of natural personal odour, odours acquired through the food the person eats as well as those precipitated by emotions and periodic odours related to reproduction. Not only is their assessment of the components of personal body odour scientifically verifiable but, unlike Western scientists, the Desana are able to describe each of the smells involved in minute and vivid detail (in Classen *et al.* 1994).

The near-world that the Ongee people of the Andaman Islands inhabit is defined by odours and not by visual features such as we normally use in constructing maps. David Howes (2006) describes it 'as fluid as the odours which animate [their] world' and asks 'how would a Western cartographer begin to map the complexities of the Ongee's fundamentally non-visual sense of place?'

In a discussion of species interaction between man and animals, David Abram (1997) takes the example of a report on a small tribe of Amazonian Indians: 'Every collective hunting expedition is preceded by careful ritual preparations, during which the hunters eat only certain foods, erasing their human odors by soaking themselves in various herbal baths and immersing themselves in the smoke of burning leaves.'

Sensitivity to human odours in non-urban communities may be much more widespread than we imagine. In conversation with a

---

[11] Classen, 1992; www.sirc.org/publik/smell_culture.html

member of the Navajo people from New Mexico, I found that she was able to detect the lingering odours of people who had previously walked along the same path.

It seems likely that people from the tribal societies described above would understand much better than we in the West what the world of a honeybee is like. The honeybee near-world is heavily dominated by odours. Not unlike the Desana communities, each hive has its own 'colony odour'. This emanates from a kind of perfumed coat worn by social insects. The coat is the wax layer that lines the tough rigid cuticle encasing the bee. Wax is a sponge for volatile compounds; they are absorbed and then released only very slowly into the boundary layer of air very close to the surface. This is still, so a bee has to push the tips of its antennae into the layer, effectively tasting the wax in order to detect the odour. The perfume is a pot-pouri of all the scents in the hive: from all the nectar brought in from various sources, volatiles from the atmosphere outside the hive (sadly this may include pesticides and pollutants), secretions from the glands of the queen and all the workers, and compounds that are constituents of bees' wax used for comb building.

There are records going back for centuries of the death's head moth entering beehives, especially the domed wicker 'skep' hives that were in use in earlier times, and plundering the honey from the combs. In 1826, William Kirby (1759–1850) and William Spence (c.1783–1860) wrote in their book *An Introduction to Entomology*:

> … long ago (in 1799) some monks who kept bees, observing they made an unusual noise, lifted the hive, when an animal flew out, which…proved to be the death's-head hawk-moth…M. Huber in 1804 discovered it had made its way into his hives, and had robbed them of their honey. In Africa we are told it has the same propensity; which the Hottentots observing, in order to monopolize the honey of wild bees, have persuaded the colonists that it inflicts a mortal wound.

In parts of the world where the moths are still common, they pose a serious threat to honey production. Now the tongue of most hawk-moths is unrolled from a coiled position to a length that enables them to feed from flowers while hovering (as in a hummingbird hawk-moth for example). In the death's head moth, in contrast, it is unusually short, in fact almost exactly the length necessary to reach to the bottom of a comb cell containing honey, and no further (Fig. 8). The tip is sharp, like the point of a tin opener, piercing the membrane covering a honey cell, and the proboscis tube is wide, enabling the moth vacuum up the viscous honey. These remarkable adaptations also make it possible for the moth to feed easily from the sticky sap oozing from damaged tree trunks.

The moths, which have very thick external skeletal casings to their bodies, usually manage to get past the trigger-happy guard bees and continue unmolested to the honeycomb. Only rarely do beekeepers find a moth that has been stung, and that seems to occur only when one has got stuck in the hive entrance. The moth makes a sound by forcing air through its proboscis (described in chapter 3) and it has been suggested that this prevents it from being attacked because it resembles the piping sound that queen honeybees use, which calms overaggressive workers and causes them to freeze. However, no one has been able to show that the voice of the moth works in this way, so the mystery requires another explanation.

The comb wax, which is secreted by glands on the abdomen of the worker honeybees, is not a pure compound but a mixture of hydrocarbons (waxes and oils) with different melting points that give it exactly the right combination of malleability and hardness for the bees to use in construction. It absorbs the same scents as the wax coat of the bees' bodies, and so the bees live, like the Ongee people, in a near-world, the extent of which is defined by smell. Different bee colonies will inevitably have different colony odours and this makes it easy for the bees to recognise intruders, whether they are bees from another colony, robber bees, wasps, hornets or other insects seeking to plunder the honey stores. So, the difference between the colony odours of two hives may be analogous to how we detect and discriminate between the odours emanating from a fish restaurant and a curry house. How, then, is the death's head moth able to enter the hive and steal the honey without being detected. The politicians' cliché of 'the elephant in the room' comes to mind: is it that the moth is a problem the bees choose to ignore because it is too big? Or can the bees for some reason not sense the presence of this creature at all, although it is elephantine to them?

In 1962, I began a research fellowship in the laboratory of Martin Lüscher at the University of Bern in Switzerland, excited by a paper published from there a few years earlier in the journal *Nature* in which a new concept was born under the name 'pheromone'. This one word was soon to become common currency among scientists and then find its way into the languages of countries throughout the world.

Peter Karlson, a biochemist from the Max Planck Institute in Munich, Germany, had studied the chemical scents that butterflies and moths use for communication and courtship, and Lüscher, a developmental biologist, had shown that termites carry substances on the outside of their bodies that determine the ratios of soldier termites, reproductive forms and workers present in a colony. The two scientists then met together and coined the term 'pheromone' (which, based on Greek roots, means 'carrier of excitation') for chemical messengers that act between individuals of the same species and act externally to the body, unlike hormones which act *within* the body (1959):

> During the past few decades, investigations have been made into various active substances which, though they resemble hormones in some respects, cannot be included among them. For example, the sexual attractants of butterflies are, like hormones, produced and secreted by special glands; minute amounts cause a specific reaction in the receptor organ (the antenna of the male), which eventually leads to a state of copulate readiness. Unlike hormones, however, the substance is not secreted into the blood but outside the body; it does not serve humoral correlation within the organism but communication between individuals.

Pheromones form the 'dark matter' that holds the universe of the honeybee colony together, the badge of identification, the instrument that gives the queen the main say over brood rearing, swarming, mating, alarm, defence and many other aspects of behaviour. The best-known pheromone, which makes the queen attractive to workers and inhibits the development of their ovaries, was discovered and identified in 1962[12] at Rothamsted Experimental Station in Harpenden (UK) by Colin G. Butler (1913–2016) and James Simpson before the pheromone concept was commonly acknowledged. Butler called it 'queen substance', although it was later found not to be a single compound but a mixture of several organic acids. This substance makes the queen irresistibly attractive to the workers and is shared by all the bees in a colony through the act of mutual licking and grooming that goes on continuously amongst the colony members. The result, as Virgil puts it in *Georgics* Book VI with a certain amount of poetic licence, is that:

> The leader is the guardian of their labours:
> to the leader they do reverence,
> and all sit round the leader in a noisy throng,
> they lift the leader on their shoulders.

We associate bees with their principal defence – their stings – and it is unsurprising that many innocuous insects, such as hoverflies, have evolved as visual mimics of honeybees.

Every year in the USA alone about forty to fifty people die from the effect of bee stings. A mass attack resulting in six hundred stings is sufficient to kill someone, but most deaths result from anaphylactic shock provoked by just a few stings. It is calculated that approximately 7 million people in the USA are hypersensitive to the venom and a single sting could be life threatening to them (Rupp, 1991).

A honeybee sting is barbed and cannot be withdrawn by the bee once it is embedded in the skin, so it is torn out from their bodies, resulting in the effective martyrdom of the bee. To make matters worse, the severed muscles around the poison sac continue to contract autonomously and force out the poisonous contents. A pheromone is released from a gland at the base of the sting when a bee is alarmed, and this continues to diffuse out from the embedded sting. The alarm pheromone is a very volatile compound – isopentylacetate – found, incidentally, in many paint stripper products, which is easy to locate against background scents and which fades

---

[12] doi.org/10.1098/rspb.1962.0009

away quickly when the danger has ceased. It focuses the attack of other workers which become very aggressive, as Virgil, again, noted in 29 BC:

> Their anger knows no bounds, and when hurt
> they suck venom into their stings, and leave their hidden lances
> fixed in the vein, laying down their lives in the wound they make.

The attacks of swarms of bees were used as an apt and brilliant metaphor by Homer in *The Iliad* for Agamemnon's men preparing for war in which the alarm pheromone becomes Zeus's crier[13]:

> …Rank and file
> Streamed behind and rushed like swarms of bees
> Pouring out of a rocky hollow, burst on endless burst
> Bunched in clusters seething over the first spring blossoms
> Dark hordes swirling into the air, this way, that way –
> …and Rumor, Zeus's crier
> like wildfire blazing among them, whipped them on.

In Greek mythology, Zeus, the ruler of the gods on Mount Olympus, owed his life to bees that defended him. Zeus was the son of Cronus, who had the disagreeable habit of eating his newborn offspring (famously depicted in Goya's shocking and horrific painting in the Museo Nacional del Prado in Madrid). Rhea, his wife, eventually lost patience with this and substituted the baby Zeus with a stone and then hid him away in a cave in Mount Ida in Crete while Cronus tucked into the stone. There, according to some accounts, the infant was fed on honey by bee maidens called *Melissae* (*Melissa* is the name for a bee in modern Greek). In gratitude, Zeus transformed the bees into stars – the Pleiades. This myth connects with a cult of bee worship in Minoan times (around 2000–1500 BC) in which the bee goddess, who is represented by contemporary engravings on gold rings and by stone carvings, was attended by women priestesses. Aggressive bees saved the infant Zeus from armed intruders, who were summoned by his guardians beating a metal drum and drove the raiders

---

[13] Homer, *The Iliad*, transl. Robert Fagles,

away with their stings. This scene is pictured on a famous Attic vase (Fig. 16), stored at the British Museum, but the 'bees' pictured there, at least to my eyes as an entomologist, are actually the species of hornet that is found in the eastern Mediterranean, which is, of course, larger and more aggressive than the honeybee. The ancient Greeks, though, following Aristotle's philosophy, had no clear species concept and grouped together all animals that had similar lifestyles and conspicuous attributes – like a sting.

I will now digress a little and discuss wax, because wax and pheromones are the key factors in the ability of the death's head moth to steal honey from bees. Waxes are remarkable substances. They repel water but absorb airborne organic molecules, including, of course, pheromones. The conquest of land in early evolution was possible only with some waterproofing cover to protect soft tissues from drying up. Terrestrial molluscs evolved methods of blocking the entrance to their calcareous shell in dry conditions. Insects developed a tough integument which also served as an external skeleton and which had a thin outer layer of soft wax that prevented water loss. As a student of zoology, I carried out the simple experiment of shaking up a tube of houseflies with carborundum powder. The powder sponges up wax, and the result is dead, desiccated flies in a matter of minutes if the atmosphere in the tube is dry. Another virtue of wax is that it helps to prevent damage of tissues by UV light; it serves this purpose also on the leaves of many trees and herbivorous plants.

Waxes and oils dissolve in each other. This has been put to good use by carnivorous pitcher plants that attract insects by scent and colour. A fly will land on the lip of the pitcher and then move downwards, feeding on sugary secretions of the plant cells. Shortly thereafter, it comes to a zone coated with microscopic wax particles that stick to Velcro-like adhesive pads on its feet. The fly can no longer get a purchase and slips and falls to its doom into the digestive juices at the bottom of the pitcher, like someone attempting to walk on an icy slope on the edge of a precipice.

Inspired by the pitcher plant, I invented a fly trap and a cockroach trap and later, realising that fine wax particles would stick to the wax on the surface of insects by electrostatic forces, I developed a new method of pest control that does not use synthetic insecticides (Howse & Underwood, 2000). Among other uses, this is now used to rid honeybees of *Varroa* parasitic mites. Electrostatically charged wax powder with essential oils dissolved in it, such as thyme oil, which is attractive to bees anyway, sticks to the mites which cannot clean it off, although the bees can. The oils in the wax then slowly kill the mites without affecting the bees. Wax formulations have also been developed which absorb synthetic pesticides. Electrostatically charged particles laced with pesticides will then stick to insects, plants and fungi, targeting them so that environmental pollution is reduced. This technique has the potential of halving the tonnage of pesticides that is used worldwide every year, but that's another story.

Back to the death's head moth. It is no accident that the moth is usually dusted with fine, white particles of wax, which, incidentally, can be shaken off dead specimens. These particles can be seen on the moth in Fig.16. When the moth first emerges from the pupa it is covered by a delicate white membrane from which the particles appear to form as the membrane dries and fragments. The guard bees in a hive pick them up when they interrogate the moth with their antennae. The particles and the rest of the surface of the body and wings are imbued with fatty acids (the kinds of compounds that are found in soap and also on the surface of skin). Although stearic acid, one of the constituents, smells of rancid butter, most other fatty acids are more or less odourless to the human nose.

When the chemical ecologists Moritz, Kirchner and Crewe (1991) took solvent extracts of the moth, they found minute traces of eight fatty acids that were present in the same recipe and in the same relative amounts in the moth as they were in the honeybees – an identical chemical signature, in other words. I reproduce the following abstract in its original form simply to show again how scientists have built up a pyramidal language to describe the world which is largely unintelligible at its summit to the layman but describes phenomena that are fascinating to those that understand it.

> Hexane extracts of *A. atropos* head, thorax, and abdomen of both males and females revealed a uniform bouquet of four dominant chemical compounds which were not substantially contaminated with solvent impurities. The mass spectra clearly identified the compounds (fit >95 %) as two unsaturated (9-hexadecenoic acid = palmitoleic acid = POA, 15 ng/µl;

9-octadecenoic acid = oleic acid = OA, 241 ng/µl) and two satu-
rated fatty acids (hexadecanoic acid = palmitic acid, 152 ng/µl;
octadecanoic acid = stearic acid = SA, 33 ng/µl). There were no
differences in the extracts of different body parts nor could we
discriminate between male and female extracts. Furthermore,
the signals from moths with hive experience were similar to
those that had never entered a bee colony. This indicates that
the compounds are not acquired from the bees but produced
by the moths. ... A typical chromatogram of a cuticular extract
of honeybees shows that the long-chain fatty acids produced by
the moth are found in a similar concentration ratio in the bee.

In a nutshell, Moritz and his colleagues had discovered that the
moths have a 'cloak of invisibility' around them, provided by the fatty
acid mixture that is identical to that which covers the body of honeybees. This is a form of chemical camouflage that enables the moth to
blend into the background of the wax combs and the bees themselves.
François Huber (1750–1831), who in 1796 published a treatise on the
honeybee, introduced a death's head moth into a nest of bumblebees
and found the poor creature was rapidly killed. The chemical PIN
recognised by honeybees is clearly not the same as that used by
bumblebees, but a death's head moth becomes just part of the pattern
on the wallpaper of scent in the darkness of the honeybee hive.

7

THE BAT'S TALE: SEEING SOUNDS

Music has colours
yellow, sunlike,
red-fingered as dawn
blue as cloudless sky at noon

Sound has light
touch has perfume
pure sound a diamond glow
broken sound the devil's tune

A bat makes piercing light
with its midnight cries
sees bright echoes
ears in the dark its eyes.

(Author)

Sensory reception and perception are two different biological concepts. It is often relatively easy to show how an animal's sense organs respond to light, sound, touch, taste or odours, and what encoded information is transmitted along nerves to the brain, but knowing how the animal experiences that information is something which we can only try to imagine. Bats are the most important predators of nocturnal moths, and to try and guess how a bat perceives a death's head moth in flight by using its ears, we need to first look at what we know about how the human brain processes information from the five senses. Many people will be surprised to learn, for example, that a few in any large crowd can actually *see* sounds as colours.

Bats are not blind; they can see but in general not very well. The expression 'blind as a bat' seems to have its origin in their ability to fly erratically around objects, swerving only at the last instant. Some are fruit eaters, for example the flying foxes; others (vampires) are blood feeders. Most species, though, feed on insects, chasing them at high speed in the night. They use ultrasonic cries like radar signals to probe the airspace in front of them for the echoes generated by flying insects. 'Black piper on an infinitesimal pipe. Little lumps that fly in air and have voices indefinite, wildly vindictive. With wings like bits of umbrella,' as D. H. Lawrence (1885–1930) described the bat in his famous 1923 poem of that name (at a time when all umbrellas were black). From the echoes, bats form a sound picture of their surroundings. To imagine what it is like to be a bat, we need to look at how, in humans, sound can give rise to pictures in the mind.

Synaesthesia manifests itself as an overlap of the senses, a kind of crosstalk in the brain. I have found by casual questioning when talking to various audiences that about two in a hundred will admit to seeing letters, words or days of the week in different colours, or even in three-dimensional space, but (like colour-blind people) never realised that they were different from all but a small number of other people in this respect. Psychiatrists see about one person in two thousand who actually complains about synaesthesia. It is found amongst people from all walks of life, including writers, artists, poets, musicians, mathematicians and scientists. Newborn babies also show symptoms of synaesthesia.

The philosopher of natural history David Abram maintains that we are all synaesthetic, though perhaps to varying degrees (1997). Thus our sensory impressions merge together: the sight of something is often coupled with a sense of smell or texture, the black marks on the page you are reading are heard as words and visual marks on a score are heard as music by most people, and familiar songs played without a singer are quickly overlain with the words in your head. More rarely, sound is associated with colour.

George Sand (1804–76), the French novelist, memoirist and socialist, was at least partially synaesthetic. In her book *Impressions et Souvenirs* (1873) she refers to conversations with the artist Eugène Delacroix (1798–1863) on the colours that they both saw in Chopin's piano music, colours that changed as it progressed to different notes and harmonies. For Delacroix, his perception of the colours was inseparable from the music, and Sand described what became known as 'Chopin's blue note', which had for her resonant transcendental properties, infusing an azure glow onto the scene. Various musicians have experienced the blue note in the composer's Nocturnes, Mazurkas and Preludes, but Chopin, try as he may, could conjure up only images of moonlight in his improvisations, which Delacroix described as only 'reflections of reflections'.

Among others, the composers Rimsky-Korsakov, Scriabin, Sibelius and Messiaen experienced synaesthesia. Their hearing and sight were married together so that they too saw vivid colours when listening to, or imagining, music. In the later nineteenth and early twentieth centuries there was a vogue of 'colour organs'. In 1911, Alexander Scriabin (1871–1915) wrote *Prometheus: The Poem of Fire*, a composition for orchestra which included a colour organ in which each key on the keyboard was tuned to produce a different colour that was projected on to a screen behind the orchestra. This was first played in New York in 1915.

The French poet Arthur Rimbaud (1854–91) was a synaesthete, although he admitted that his poem *Voyelles* was partly an invention. It begins:

A black, E white, L red, U green, O blue: vowels,
I will explain some day your latent origins:
A, black velvet corset of exploding insects
Which buzz around cruel stenches.

The writer Vladimir Nabokov (1899–1977) presented with what he called 'a fine case of coloured hearing'. While thinking about the sound of a letter and imagining its outline he would see it in colour. In his autobiography *Speak, Memory* (1951) he described, in vivid language, similar to that used by Rimbaud and Proust, the precise impressions that his senses gave to him; for example:

Oatmeal n, noodle-limp l, and the ivory-backed hand mirror of o take care of the whites. I am puzzled by my French on which I see as the brimming tension-surface of alcohol in a small glass.' and '…m is a fold of pink flannel, and today I have at last perfectly matched with 'Rose Quartz' in Maerz and Paul's Dictionary of Color.

Some composers have an exceptional ability to evoke a sound picture. I myself cannot fail to sense the strength and majesty of *The Bogatyr Gates of Kiev* from the movement in Modest Mussorgsky's (1839–81) *Pictures at an exhibition*. Bedřich Smetana's (1824–84) set of tone poems entitled *Má Vlast* (My Homeland) is a masterpiece of sound-painting. The most famous of these is *Vltava* (The Moldau), in which he evokes, through the music, scenes of the Bohemian river as it flows from a trickle at its source to the junction with the Elbe in Prague, including a farmer's wedding, the round dance of mermaids in moonlight, and castles, ruins and palaces above the swirling river.

A wonderful image in the form of light, colour, texture, touch and sound is conjured up by Pablo Neruda's (1904–73) poem *Ode to the Piano* (describing a music recital) in which the following lines create an impression of synaesthesia:

the sweetness slid like rain over a bell….
an emerald went across the abyss…
the structure of the rose sang.

Again, in *The Ships* he switches capriciously between sensory modes of colour, sound and movement:

With ardent colour of gilt boxes
Which cinnamon had made resound like violins,
…
The green welcome suavities
Of jades, and the pallid cereal of silk,
Everything scrolled on the sea like a voyage of wind,
Like a dance of disappearing anemonies.

There is a problem with the diagnosis of synaesthesia. It can be very difficult to know whether or not someone who appears to be synaesthetic is drawing on their imagination or relying on familiar associations – for example the word 'sky' may trigger an image of blue in the mind or whether the association is an inborn attribute from which a person cannot escape.

From the blind Homer onwards, who is relying on metaphor in the following passage from the *Odyssey*, poets have tended to associate dawn with slowly changing colours:

> Dawn with her rose-red fingers might have shone
> upon their tears, if with her glinting eyes
> Athena…held back the night, and night lingered long
> at the western edge of the earth, while in the east
> she reined in Dawn of the golden throne at Ocean's banks.

Most composers of music associate the changing light of dawn with a slow, peaceful awakening, as Edvard Grieg does in *Morning* from his *Peer Gynt* Suite and Benjamin Britten in his evocative first *Sea Interlude* from the opera *Peter Grimes*. Rudyard Kipling, however, in *The Road to Mandalay*, described it as sound: 'An' the dawn comes up like thunder outer China 'crost the Bay' and the thunder crescendos in the once popular song based on this poem.

Reviews of Marcel Proust's much-quoted association of memories produced by the taste of a madeleine (rather than its appearance) usually overlook other strong indications of synaesthesia in his writing on place names in *Remembrance of Times Past*. The name of Parma, for example, was to him 'compact, smooth, violet-tinted and soft', and Pont-Aven 'pink-white flash of the wing of a lightly posed coif, tremulously reflected in the greenish waters of a canal.' Proust was known to be an avid drug user, however, and such impressions may have been drug induced and temporary. This is hinted at in the following extract in *In Search of Lost Time III: The Guermantes Way* (1931):

> Not far thence is the secret garden in which kinds of sleep, so
> different from one another, induced by datura, by Indian hemp,
> by the multiple extracts of ether – the sleep of belladonna, of

opium, of Valerian – grow like unknown flowers whose petals remain closed until the day when the predestined stranger comes to open them with a touch and to liberate for long hours the aroma of their peculiar dreams for the delectation of an amazed and spellbound being…

The philosopher John Locke (1632–1704) was probably the first to describe the phenomenon of transposition of sound and colour in a blind man, which he mentions in *An Essay Concerning Human Understanding* (1690):

> A studious blind man who had mightily beat his head about a visible objects, and made use of the explanation of his books and friends, to understand the names of light and colours which often came in his way, bragged one day, that he now understood what scarlet signified. Upon which his friend demanding what scarlet was? the blind man answered, it was like the sound of a trumpet.

The highly original French, twentieth-century composer Olivier Messiaen (1908–92) wrote descriptions of the colours of chords, ranging from the simple 'gold and brown' to the more psychedelic 'blue-violet rocks, speckled with little grey cubes, cobalt blue, deep Prussian blue, highlighted by a bit of violet-purple, gold, red, ruby, and stars of mauve, black and white. Blue-violet is dominant!' He even put marginal notes on the scores of certain of his compositions to aid the conductor in interpretation (presumably a vain hope for most). In an interview he said:

> Sounds are high, low, fast, slow etc. My colours do the same thing, they move in the same way. Like rainbows shifting from one hue to the next. … They're musician's colours, not to be confused with painter's colours. They're colours that go with music. If you tried to reproduce these colours on canvas it may produce something horrible. They're not made for that, they're musician's colours.

He added, referring to complementary colours which he thought were produced in a similar way to the sounds of chords,

'I have a red carpet that I often look at. Where this carpet meets the lighter-coloured parquet next to it, I intermittently see marvelous greens that a painter couldn't mix – natural colours created in the eye.'

Frances Wilson, writing as 'The Cross-eyed Pianist', would understand this perfectly, being a synaesthete[14]. Each key in music has for her a different colour: C is brick-red, D is sky-blue, E is orange etc.

In Chopin's Etude Opus 10 no 3…the chromatic passages in augmented 4ths in the stormy middle section of the piece are a riot of almost psychedelic colour as well as sound… This piece is mostly orange, green and red.

Music is sometimes transposed into visual art – and back again. The French artist Tini Noy colours her paintings and portraits with the colours evoked by listening to music while working in her atelier. Another artist, Anne Salz, also explains on her website how the music she listens to while painting rewrites the colours and brush strokes into something little like a fluid musical score representing the impressions she receives. Both these artists then hear the music that originated the paintings when they look at the painting subsequently.

Anthropologists have discovered that the sensory world of members of Amazonian tribes, such as the Desana, is one in which overlap between different modalities is the rule rather than the exception. Anthropologist David Howes, reviewing this with reference to the work of G. Reichel-Dolmatoff, mentions that the Desana delight in cross-sensory associations (in Classen *et al.* 1994). When a boy plays a flute:

The odor of the tune is said to be male, the color is red, and the temperature is hot; the tune evokes youthful happiness and the taste of a fleshy fruit of a certain tree. The vibrations carry an erotic message to a particular girl.

---

[14] www.crosseyedpianist.com/about/

The variety of sensory worlds in different human beings, aspects of that of one person being almost impossible to imagine from the viewpoint of another[15], makes it even more difficult for us to know how an animal perceives the world. Scientific dogma avoids this issue: anthropomorphism has long been a cardinal sin amongst students of animal behaviour but scientific investigation nevertheless usually proceeds under the assumption that man is totally superior in faculties. William Shakespeare's *Hamlet* recognised the arrogance of such an opinion when in a cynical frame of mind:

> What a piece of work is a man! How noble in reason, how infinite in faculty! In form and moving how express and admirable! In action how like an angel, in apprehension how like a god! The beauty of the world. the paragon of animals.

We have little inkling of whether animals are synaesthetes and whether, as in Locke's blind man, sounds evoke colour for them. It would be a marvelous economy of nature if a male robin heard another's song in red, a yellowhammer heard yellow or if a nightingale's song were fawn in colour and feather textured. Or, to turn this on its head, whether a red breast evokes one or other of the vocalisations of another robin, and so forth. A hint that colour sensations can be attached to animal sounds comes from Jamie Ward's book *The Frog Who Croaked Blue* (2008). The title was inspired by the innocent question of a synaesthetic child who, listening to the calls of frogs, wanted to know what the blue-croaker and the white-croaker were.

Neurophysiologists have found that nerves, so-called transient cortical projections, connect the auditory and visual processing centres of the human brain, which is circumstantial evidence for the splicing together of sensory impressions. The transient cortical projections have also been found in ferrets, monkeys and cats, and are, as the name implies, lost within a few months. In newborn babies the evidence is that the cortical projections respond initially to the overall intensity of stimulation from all the senses, but two to three weeks after birth this amalgam of sensory impressions separates out into

---

[15] For further details see Baron-Cohen & Harrison, 1997

different modalities as the transient connections in the brain are lost. In rodents, however, these connections persist into adult life[16], suggesting that this is the more primitive condition and therefore that the echolocation system of bats may have evolved from a synaesthetic condition. Pigeons also have cross connections between the auditory and visual brain centres.

The phenomenon of synaesthesia raises interesting questions that at first seem comical. Do bats hear in colour? If so, is it what we know as colour? Do they hear shapes? We do know that some synaesthetes see not just patches of colour known as 'photisms' but also coloured shapes. This reinforces the selectionist theory of colour perception – intuitively difficult for us to grasp – that colour is generated in the mind and is not a property of pigments or the wavelength of reflected light[17].

The concept of sound making a 'picture' makes one wonder whether animals see the kinds of colours that Messiaen saw. Insectivorous bats such as pipistrelles broadcast brief ultrasonic clicks that sweep down in pitch, and the horseshoe bats emit a longer note of fixed wavelength (i.e. pitch). In either case, the returning echo from an object is matched with the outgoing cry, so the bat will hear briefly a chord. That chord will locate the object in space and time for the bat. This is how neurophysiologists describe this phenomenon (Ulanovsky & Moss, 2008):

> The bat computes the horizontal and vertical positions of targets from differences in the perceived arrival time, intensity, and spectrum of echoes at the two ears… The bat estimates target range from the time delay between the outgoing vocalization and returning echo; some bat species show extraordinary spatial discrimination along the range axis, with thresholds for range changes <0.1 mm. … the bat perceives the size of an object from the intensity of echoes, the target velocity from the Doppler shift of the echoes, and the object's shape from the spectrum of the echoes. In fact, bats are able to use their sonar for high-level perceptual tasks such as object recognition

---

[16] See for example Jack *et al.* 2013

[17] For a discussion of this controversial issue see Allen, 2009

and classification and even for texture discrimination, e.g., the roughness of surfaces.

From the bat's perspective we can imagine that the echoes from the acoustic searchlight that the bat broadcasts are transmitted on to a screen in the mind in the form of patterns of brightness. As a bright image shows up, the bat increases the rate of its high-pitched cries, which if they were in our hearing range would sound like a motorcycle revving up, and the sound would be as deafening as a machine gun firing. The bat is not deafened by its own cries, which are muted by its ears at the precise moment the cries are emitted and then the sensitivity is immediately reset to the sound frequency of echoes.

The American biologist Kenneth D. Roeder began his research into the hearing of moths after a strange experience at a barbecue in the early evening. Moths were hovering around lanterns in the garden when someone made a high-pitched sound by rubbing their fingers across the rim of a wine glass. Suddenly moths dropped to the ground. Had the sound energy killed them? Was this a phenomenon similar to a wine glass shattering when resonating to a powerful baritone voice? No – they quickly recovered, but each time the sound was repeated they fell again.

Roeder and his colleague Asher Treat found that some moths, especially those belonging to the family Arctiidae, which includes tiger moths that are often brightly coloured and sometimes day-flying, possess a pair of eardrums on the first segment of the abdomen. These moths are generally poisonous. In responding to the echolocation calls of bats they have anticipated the performance of Spitfire fighter planes in the Second World War. In dogfights, British Spitfire pilots would escape from German Messerschmitt 109s by diving towards the ground and pulling up at the last moment at very high g-forces, knowing that the less manoeuvrable German planes would find it much harder to pull back and avoid disaster.

The death's head moth, curiously, hears with its mouthparts (Göpfert & Wasserthal, 1999). The small, paired, finger-like appendages at the base of the proboscis interlock with each other and form a kind of miniature receiving antenna that activates sense cells within them. These bizarre ears are used in evading bats by variations on the Spitfire technique or by producing their own acoustic counter-measures. The moths respond to sounds up to 100 kHz, five times the upper frequency, detectable by the most sensitive human ears but similar to the frequency of calls from echolocating bats. Their simple ears, each innervated by just two nerve endings, are tuned to the ultrasound cries of moths. When one nerve cell is stimulated by ultra-sound, the moth starts to change its trajectory in flight, but when the second cell becomes activated by more intense sound pulses, the moth immediately drops down, dives or carries out aerobatic manoeuvres designed to take it very quickly out of the path of an approaching bat.

When a moth hears the bat sonar pulses, it immediately produces its own sounds (Barber & Kawahara, 2013) that contain ultrasonic components with similar characteristics to those of insectivorous bats. These may startle bats, warn them that the moth is distasteful or confuse them by introducing false echoes. There is a recorded obser-vation of a moth responding to the approach of two bats with cries that effectively frightened the bats away.

An ultrasonic defence system was revealed in tiger moths by two British biologists, David Pye and Gillian Sales (1974), who recorded ultrasound clicks given off by these moths when recordings of echo-locating bats were played to them. At the base of the third leg of the moth they found a blister-like area of the cuticle (the hard, outer skele-ton of insects). An internal muscle can bend this in and then release it, as you might do with the lid of a tin can or with a clicker used for training dogs. The clicks contain ultrasonic frequencies, but those of moths actually come in a fast train, like the sound of a zip being undone. And that is roughly how they are produced: each buckling membrane has a zone down the middle with ridges like those on a file so that the click fragments into a succession of clicks as each space between the ridges buckles in and out separately. This sound is believed to jam the bat's sonar with confusing 'noise', but it may have another effect. To the bat the false echoes must appear like a barrage of screaming sparks, while a death's head moth will throw off the equivalent of a Klaxon signal, followed, if caught, by a bit-ter corrosive taste in the bat's mouth and pain from the sharp spines on the moth's legs. Other moths will then be better defended if the bat learns the association between the moth's sound signals and its distastefulness.

Echoes from scattered sound fill a screen in the mind
transmuted into points of light – myriad megapixels
Ahead, sound from the acoustic searchlight rebounds,
creating sparkling meteor shower from flying insects.
Flying towards it, one image glows brighter and larger,
The rate of sharp high-pitched cries gathers and grows-
deafening as machine guns are to sensitive ears
like the vibrating crescendo you hear from a racing bike.
Cries fired away are veiled to protect the ears,
Then lifted in the next splinter of a second
receiving the echo's new view of what lies ahead.
Suddenly the echo fades,
Dropping through the air.
A quick sweep of the wing,
like the flick of a whip –
The insect is in the mouth.

(Author)

When a death's head moth hears the sonar pulses of the bat, it immediately produces its own sounds by a completely different and bizarre method. The sounds were previously thought to come from the proboscis (see Chapter 3), but biologists have found an extraordinary method of sound generation that is widespread in hawk-moths: the ultrasonic sounds come from the genitalia (Barber & Kawahara, 2013). Flaps protecting the genital opening at the tip of the abdomen have rows of hard scales on them, and the sounds are produced by rubbing these flaps together, rather in the manner of a stiff piece of plastic rubbed over a file. Reporters in the national press vied with one another in thinking up amusing titles for their articles, including 'Hawkmoths squeak their genitals at threatening bats and the more down-to-earth Ultrasonic bollock blasters help Hawkmoth battle the Bat', while the journal *Nature* posted 'Hawkmoths zap bats with sonic blasts from their genitals.' The Natural History Museum in London showed more decorum with *Moths and Bats: An Evolutionary War*. This 'war' or 'evolutionary arms race', as many biologists like to call it, began, researchers have concluded (Kawahara & Barber, 2015), with the ability of many species groups of hawk-moths to produce ultrasound, starting in the late Oligocene (~26 mya) after the emergence of insectivorous bats. Sonar jamming and bat-detecting ears arose in the Miocene (18–14 mya), so it is likely that the death's head hawkmoth has been co-evolving to combat the attentions of bats for a very long of time.

Like most moths and butterflies, the death's head moth has evolved resistance to the toxins in its food-plants (including, as we have seen, potatoes). As a caterpillar, it sequesters them in its body tissues and uses them for its own protection. Once in the body they stay there, through metamorphosis to the adult moth as the following researchers (Nash *et al.* 1993) found:

> Polyhydroxylated tropane alkaloids, not hitherto recorded from the potato (*Solanum tuberosum*), were detected in the leaves and tubers of this plant. They are potent inhibitors of glycosidases and may be responsible for neurological disorders in livestock. These alkaloids were also extracted from a sphingid moth…the larvae of which feed on *Solanum*.

Moths have other defences against bats. The wings and bodies of many species are covered in long hairs which provide good insulation and absorb sound, hence muffling the reflected echo of the bat ultrasound cries. In addition, moth wing scales, unlike those of butterflies, are honey-combed with air pockets, a feature also of sound-absorbent foam used in echo chambers. The scales are most absorbent at the ultrasonic frequencies that most bats use, suggesting that they have evolved stealth techniques that make them less conspicuous to bats (Zeng *et al.*, 2011). By flying close to trees and bushes, moths make detection by bats even more difficult because of the numerous echoes from leaves.

8

THE BIRD'S TALE

Who knows how a robin sees
the sunlight's hues a raindrop frees?
What shapes are reborn in a falcon's eye?
phantoms unknown to you and I.
What beauty is hidden from our view
in birds, butterflies, and morning dew?

(Author)

For many years biologists have been investigating the ways in which birds communicate visually and their methods of selecting prey on the assumption that they see colours and shapes in the same way that we do. This seems reasonable enough when it has been possible to show that some birds have both good colour vision and excellent visual acuity, several times better than ours in the case of eagles (Shlaer, 1972).

In the middle of the twentieth century a great deal of research was carried out on homing pigeons and other migratory birds leading to conclusions that many species use the sun as a compass. This requires an internal clock to compensate for the sun's movements across the sky during the day. But this only accounts for their direction finding; earlier, most researchers accepted that point-to-point navigation in homing pigeons, for example, must depend upon either some means of measuring the rate of change of the sun's arc or calculating the noon-day position of the sun where they are and comparing these co-ordinates with the location of the home loft – rather a lot, it seems, to ask of a bird. Now, half a century later, it is known that birds have a magnetic sense that may generate visual patterns giving indications of the earth's magnetic field or that, alternatively, they rely on receptors located in the inner ear – in which case they may hear it. (This, however, needs qualification, because the nervous input from sensory organs goes to a region in the brain where nerves from the eye, or from the ear, eventually end up.) We have, though, no evidence whatever that a bird 'sees' or 'hears' as we do – we can assume only that they experience some kind of sensation. Homing pigeons can detect the magnetic field's direction, intensity and polarity, which strongly suggests that they have their own GPS system, but in what form they perceive this is probably unanswerable[18].

We have little means of knowing what a bird sees, and neither can we but hazard a guess as to what the next person sees. It is, though, not disputed that birds see a rainbow that is different from the one we see, and that most species can also see UV light which is normally invisible to us. Most nocturnal animals do not see a colour rainbow at all. A striking exception to this, curiously enough, is found in hawk-moths (Land & Osorio, 2003), including the elephant hawk-moth, *Deilephila elpenor* that can see spectral colours at night at light intensities where humans are completely colour blind and see only shades of grey. They cannot, though, detect changes in brightness.

The structure and physiology of insect eyes is completely different from that of vertebrates, and colour vision in the latter would not be useful at night because colour-detecting sensory cells – the cones of the vertebrate retina – are hundred times less sensitive to light than the rods which do not detect colour. It has been estimated that animals that have one cone in the retina can see about 100 shades of grey, which would give no evolutionary advantage over the possession of rods, but when two types of cone are present it is possible to see a spectrum of colour.

We normally have three types of cone in the retina of the eye, each sensitive to light of a different and limited range of wavelengths, and with that combination we see seven to eight different colour bands in

---

[18] See: Pigeons may 'hear' magnetic fields: Daniel Cressey (2012), www .nature.com/news/pigeons-may-hear-magnetic-fields-1.10540

a rainbow – the three primary colours of red, blue and green – and as a result of the overlap of sensitivity of these we also see orange, yellow, indigo and violet. Colour-blind people, specifically those with only two-cone types, see only five colour bands in total. However, an estimated three to fifty per cent of women (depending on their racial origins) and up to eight per cent of men have 4-cone vision and, depending on their genetic constitution, can distinguish ten colour bands in a rainbow (Jameson *et al.*, 2001).

We see light reflected from the objects around us rarely as a pure colour as it is at different points on a rainbow or spectrum but as a mixture of colours in varying proportions. It is claimed that the addition of each extra cone results in the perception of hundred times more hues because of the overlap of responsiveness of the different cones to light of mixed wavelength. The human eye, then, is theoretically capable of discriminating, at a conservative estimate, about 1 million hues and in the case of the (4-cone) tetrachromats 100 million. This suggests, incidentally, that artistic ability and art appreciation may be better developed amongst certain sectors of the population as is the attribute of perfect pitch in relation to hearing.

One study in America has revealed that around half of all women have a fourth colour cone in the retina, implying that they can see hundred times more hues than ninety-seven per cent of men that have the standard RGB cones. Gloria Moss (2014) has found that this is linked in some way to significant differences in perception of colour and design between men and women. Men greatly prefer designs created by men, and women prefer designs made by women. Men prefer lots of straight lines, while women prefer busy pictures with lots of curved lines. I suddenly found myself looking at a picture hanging in my study of stylised butterflies painted by a local artist. The wings have a lot of straight lines running across them and the wing borders are straight edged. Sure enough, it was painted by a man (my wife doesn't like it much). Apart from obvious disparities in seeing, Moss argues that these gender differences have their origin in the hunter-gatherer activity that occupied men and women for ninety-nine per cent of human history. Thus, the ability to form a cognitive map of largely featureless surroundings is essential for hunters, while women are more adept at spotting and collecting berries, nuts and fruit without straying far from home and family.

The blue cone in the human eye can also detect UV light, but because of its shorter wavelength it is mostly reflected from the cornea and the lens in the eye. In the eye condition known as aphakia the lens is lacking, and people thus affected can see UV as a bright white light tinged with blue or violet. Those who have had the lens removed and replaced with a crystalline lens that allows the passage of some UV light report disturbances in their perception of colour, giving a violet tinge to black and other colours. A fascinating description of UV perception is given by Alan Bradley, a Canadian academic. After a cataract operation during which his surgeon had implanted a plastic lens (transparent to UV light) in his left eye, he was startled to find that he was seeing very bright reflections, and when he arrived at a produce market one day, he was overwhelmed by a brilliant mauve light. 'It was almost as though I had been hit on the nose,' he says. 'It was like listening to a Mozart symphony in one ear in the key of C and in the other in the key of D, I had to look away.' The effect was generated by blacklight sources that the market traders used to identify forged banknotes by checking for watermarks[19]. Banknotes and credit cards are commonly marked with pigments or microstructures that fluoresce under UV light, reflecting it back at a somewhat longer wavelength in the normal visual range. Such pigments are also used in some washing powders to make white clothing appear whiter (with the added result that they fluoresce under the blacklight sources used in night clubs).

William S. Stark, a scientist who had a lens removed from one eye, found that he could detect UV with wavelengths down to 305 nm, almost at the limits at which sunlight can penetrate the atmosphere (1987). This again suggests that UV is a more primitive condition in evolution and that the lens in the eye evolved a filtering mechanism to prevent progressive damage to the retina from sunlight.

Most birds are also tetrachromats, but the retina differs from that in humans because the distribution of peak sensitivities is different. Birds have a cone which has peak sensitivity in the UV range (at 370 nanometres) so the peaks are at 370–445 and 508–565 nm, compared with 430–550–570 nm in humans with 3-cone types. This means that the colour bands they see in a spectrum will be in a different array

---

[19] Reported in *Fortune Magazine* by Ivan Amato, 'Bird's Eye View' (2005)

from those we see, with boundaries at different wavelengths between whatever 'colours' they see. It is an assumption, of course, that birds see colours we experience or whether they see something analogous. The implications of tetrachromacy are that birds *may* see hundred times more hues than most people can, that the colour boundaries will be in different positions and UV reflections to which we all are almost insensitive will be seen by birds.

Colours have effects upon human emotions and are often linked to them semantically, as we see in Viola's comment about her fictional sister in Shakespeare's *Twelfth Night*:

> …: she pined in thought,
> And with a green and yellow melancholy
> She sat like patience on a monument,
> Smiling at grief. Was not this love indeed?

The large canvasses of the artist Mark Rothko (1903–1970) have a powerful, numinous effect on many people. His *Seagram murals* in the Tate Gallery in London, consisting of large expanses of maroon, purple and black that intergrade into one another, have been counted among the most powerful of all twentieth-century paintings and according to one critic 'make you stop and look intently with a strange mixture of melancholy and fulfilment'.

In contrast, the blue-violet end of the colour spectrum is a numinous zone. Purple[20] and violet are colours that are often associated with psychedelia, authority, distinction and extravagance. In the Hindu Buddhist religion, the chakras are assigned different colours: the head chakra, which is associated with mysticism, visual consciousness and clarity of mind is purple, indigo or blue. People following Eastern meditation practices sometimes report a purple aura.

Ovid (43 BC–17 AD)[21] records that King Minos of Cretan mythology fought with King Nisus of Megara, which lies on the shores of the Corinth canal. Nisus had a bright purple tress of hair, the talismanic

---

[20] Words for colours are often not equivalent in different languages. Thus, the French *poupre* refers to a more reddish colour than the English purple. See: Mollard-Desfour, 2008

[21] Ovid, *Metamorphoses* Book V111

properties of which made him invincible. His daughter, however, fell in love with King Minos and cut off her father's purple lock of hair, allowing Minos to conquer the city.

Purple was associated with power in ancient Rome: it was worn by Emperors and the aristocracy whose garments were coloured with the extremely expensive dye that was extracted from marine molluscs. Still a symbol of power today, it is particularly associated with senior church clerics, members of the legal profession and royalty. The Purple Heart is one of the United States' most prestigious military decorations, originally established by George Washington and awarded, among others, to John F Kennedy.

The Irish poet W. B. Yeats (1865–1939), in his vision of *The Lake Isle of Innisfree*, uses the colour purple to convey a sense of spiritual tranquillity:

> Dropping from the veils of the morning to where the cricket sings;
> There midnight's all a glimmer, and noon a purple glow,
> And evening full of linnet's wings.

Violet also has strong spiritual connotations. Violets were used by the Romans on graves as a symbol of affection for the departed, in mediaeval folklore as a protection against evil spirits and in later times as a token of love. In his sonnet in praise of blue colours Keats wrote[22]:

> Blue! … – and, that Queen
> Of secrecy, the Violet: what strange powers
> Hast thou, as a mere shadow! But how great,
> When in an Eye thou art, alive with fate!

Violet is a spectral colour – part of the rainbow, while purple is not and is produced from a mixture of blue and red. Violet, as with other colours of the spectrum, appears different in high-light intensity, seeming more blue in this case, while purple does not. Purple colours are commonly seen in the disorder known as Charles Bonnet Syndrome, in which people suffer hallucinations. This is believed to be

---

[22] In 'St Agnes Eve' by John Keats

due to distortions of the information in the pathways from the retina to the visual lobe of the brain, in which the brain fills the vacuum with images that can be frightening for the sufferer. It has been described as follows (Sachs, 2012):

> CBS (Charles Bonnet Syndrome) hallucinations are often described as having dazzling, intense colour or a fineness and richness of detail far beyond anything one sees with the eyes… perhaps the most common are phosphemes, blobs or clouds of brightness or colour, which may or may not differentiate into anything more complex.

The hypothesis that our sense organs filter out information that we could otherwise visualise originates from the writer Aldous Huxley, author of the famous satire on behaviourism and the power of behavioural conditioning, *Brave New World*. In 1953, Huxley, who was well versed in Eastern mysticism and philosophy, took the hallucinogenic drug mescaline as an experiment. This, like LSD, which he took subsequently, produced amazing and radical changes in his visual perception which he described in *The Doors of Perception*, the title taken from Williams Blake's poem *The Marriage of Heaven and Hell*:

> If the doors of perception were cleansed every thing would appear to man as it is, infinite. For man has closed himself up, till he sees all things through narrow chinks of his cavern[23].

Interestingly, Huxley saw purple colours where none are normally seen. Such colours dominate psychedelic art in which all colours are typically very bright, strong in colour contrast and rich in flowing designs. In *The Doors of Perception* (1954) he wrote:

> That chair – shall I ever forget it? Where the shadows fell on the canvas upholstery, stripes of a deep but glowing indigo

---

[23] Blake may have had in mind the allegory of Plato's Cave, in which Plato pictured the effect of education on the ability of someone to see more and more of reality as they were drawn out of their 'cave' of ignorance.

alternated with stripes of an incandescence so intensely bright that it was hard to believe that they could be made of anything but blue fire. … The event was this succession of azure furnace doors separated by gulfs of unfathomable gentian. It was inexpressibly wonderful, wonderful to the point, almost, of being terrifying.

Huxley's experience with mescaline led him to his *Mind at Large* theory, indicating that the brain is capable of perceiving everything but can function only by filtering out what is not relevant to human existence. He concluded that the brain protects us from being overwhelmed and confused by 'a mass of largely useless and irrelevant knowledge' leaving only a selection that may be practically useful.

The concept of sensory filtering has also been of use in ethology, the scientific study of animal behaviour, where, as we have already seen, sense organs respond to only selective parts of the auditory and electromagnetic spectrum. The view that during the course of evolution man evolved sensory filters to stop damaging levels of UV light entering the eyes matches well with that of Huxley: i.e. that we can perceive UV as long as the appropriate part of the visual lobe of the brain is stimulated by nerve input or drugs.

When early hominids left the forest environment, they were more exposed to the damaging effects of the sun's rays on their eyes and exposed skin surfaces, which can easily lead to skin cancer. This would have been countered by the evolution of a filter in the lens, acting like a volume control on the sensory messages from the retina to the brain. It has been suggested that hair was lost in early man (except on the head) because the need for cooling the skin became paramount, which is more easily achieved by transpiration of water from the sweat glands and evaporation on the skin. That left the skin vulnerable to damage by UV light, a problem that was solved by the pigment melanin. If you need convincing of the need to protect skin, look at your dog or cat, if you have one. It is covered by a thick hair coat – even on its eyelids and outer ears. The exposed skin of the nose and lips is coloured dark brown, or even black, coated with a cutaneous armour of melanin with no chinks in it. In some long-nosed breeds, however, there is a small gap between the brown nose and the fur of the snout. Such animals are susceptible to skin cancer, particularly in places with very sunny climates such as Australia.

Melanin is a remarkable molecule without which the evolution of life on land would have taken a very different course and we might all have been Neanderthal-like troglodytes. A screen of melanin would have been especially important during Ice Ages: the reflectance of light from snow is seventy to eighty per cent while that from forests is only ten per cent. Interestingly, Neanderthals had orbits which were substantially larger than in *Homo sapiens*, possibly because they were adapted to hunting for food in low light conditions of forests.

Melanin has been found in the feathers of the pretentiously named *Confuciusornis sanctus* (holy bird of Confucius) from 120 mya, which had very dark plumage on its head (Zhang, 2010), and melanin, of course, is present in human skin and in the iris of the eye. It absorbs UV light and converts 99.99 per cent of the energy into light of very long wavelength, beyond the visible red spectrum, hence into heat. Melanin is found in the feathers of birds, in special cells known as melanocytes. In the male peacock bird the spacing between the stacks of melanocytes produces a microscopic grid that reflects and refracts light as it does from a thin film of oil, or the surface of a CD held in sunlight, creating brilliant iridescent colours that change as the angle of reflected light and the thickness of the film changes. The melanin provides a dark background to the sheen and the transparent feather structure scatters the coloured light.

While writing this, I am looking at the fronds of a palm tree in the sun. Of course, they are all green but only because of preconceptions which my brain has instilled. Looking more carefully, I can see, as in a stilled digital photographic image, that some foliage is dark green, some light green, some black and some white, depending on the light that is reflected from them. At dawn and dusk with more red light in the sky the palm appears still green, but the digital image from my camera says otherwise. This phenomenon of static colour perception is known as colour constancy. There is no unequivocal evidence that animals have this, and if not, it may be that birds live in a psychedelic world of constantly changing colours – the visual equivalent of music – as we see on iridescent feathers and on the wings of morpho butterflies, and on the surface of a CD as we turn it this and that way. As the philosopher Keith Allen has pointed out (2009) that we perceive colours against the background of a stably coloured world, but if all colours were perceived against a background of ephemeral colours, the world would seem very different from the one we know. In the end we have to conclude that to know what another person or another species experiences as colour is as inaccessible to science as the music of Mozart is to a grasshopper.

The experience of blind people shortly after they have had their sight restored confirms that much of the perception of visual images in otherwise normal subjects has to be learnt. Colour is seen as a property, detached from objects and with no spatial location, scarlet having the most impact on the senses; the shape and form of objects must be learnt before they can be recognised subsequently, and the size of objects is not correlated with distance from the eye (Gregory & Wallace, 1963)

In 1947 the now renowned ornithologist and ecologist David Lack (1910–73) published a little book entitled *The Life of the Robin* (1943) in which he recorded his experiments on the territoriality of robins, which showed that the song of the robin did not serve, as was generally believed then, solely to advertise for a mate but was also a warning to rival males near his territory to keep away. A male in his territory, Lack found, would attack stuffed male robins, and even a bunch of red feathers, as readily as it would other live males. On one occasion a robin attacked the empty space where the red feathers had been! Lack wrote:

> The world of a robin is so strange and remote from our experience that into it we can scarcely penetrate, except to see dimly how different it must be from our own.

Evidently, robins, like newly resighted blind people, see the red colour detached from the form of the bird. The founding fathers of ethology (the scientific study of animal behaviour), who were also Nobel laureates, Konrad Lorenz (1903–89) and Nikolaas Tinbergen, subsequently found other instances in which perception of colour in birds appeared to be dissociated from form. Lorenz is remembered by biologists and non-specialists alike for his engaging accounts, described in his book *King Solomon's Ring*, of the behaviour of animals with which he shared his life (1961). He showed, for example, how duck-lings and goslings become imprinted on their parents and follow them around. Young birds reared without natural parents would 'see' any familiar object as the parent (irrespective of its shape or colour): an empty box, or Lorenz himself.

Lorenz got most pleasure and possibly most of his insights from observing his tame jackdaws. Recognition of an enemy, he explained, is learnt by tradition in jackdaws, by handing down the information from one generation to the next and 'any living being that carried a black thing, dangling or fluttering, becomes the object of a furious onslaught.' Lorenz tells the story of his return from a swim in the Danube, when he went to the loft to call his jackdaws home and lock them up for the night:

> I suddenly felt something wet and cold in my trouser pocket into which, in a hurry, I had pushed my black bathing drawers. I pulled them out – and the next moment was surrounded by a dense cloud of raging, rattling jackdaws, which hailed agoniz-ing pecks at my offending hand.

The black colour had been the trigger, independent of its form, for the attack. The birds had perceived a jackdaw in the grasp of a preda-tor and the lack of wings, a beak eyes, feet, etc., was not 'seen'.

It is, to me at least, rather sad that Konrad Lorenz's illuminating anecdotes and simple experiments found little favour in the succeed-ing generation of ethologists and have been confined to the vaults of biological thought. The main reason is that the concepts of instinct and 'drives' that he borrowed from Freud and used in his conceptual models of the organisation of animal behaviour were seen as nothing more than metaphors for physiological processes and unhelpful in that they introduced arbitrary dichotomies, separating instinct from learning rather than allowing for any grey areas arising from subtle developmental processes. Lorenz stuck to his guns, maintaining that stereotyped behaviour patterns were under purely genetic control with a hard core of fixed automatism (1965). (This, of course, is no dif-ferent from the current and universally accepted view of neurologists that behaviour is either 'hard-wired' or learnt.) The anthropomorphism of Lorenz was also regarded with suspicion by scientists, but he made no apology for this. Referring to writers of animal stories, including Kipling, he wrote:

> …poets such as the authors of these books may well avail themselves of poetic licence to present the animal in a way far diverged from the scientific truth. They may daringly let the animal speak like a human being, they may even ascribe human motives to its actions, and yet succeed in retaining the general style of the wild creature. Surprisingly enough, they convey a true impression of what a wild animal is like, although they are telling fairy tales.

Thomas H. Huxley (1825–95), the Victorian evolutionist who earned himself the title of 'Darwin's bulldog', expressed a similar view that no scientist should ignore: 'In scientific work, those who refuse to go beyond fact rarely get as far as fact.' Once more you are thinking I have digressed, but Lack, Lorenz and Tinbergen were the first to understand that only certain details of the image that falls on the retina of the bird's eye are used to generate an image in its brain. It was Tinbergen (1951) who found a metaphor for this; he called the usually simple configurations of detail, including patches of colour that would pass through the birds' doors of perception and trigger a behavioural response, 'sign stimuli'.

The death's head moth has a large body. Some of the fuel for its powerful flight muscles comes from the energy-rich honey and fruit sugars it consumes that are stored in the body and allow it to fly fast and for long distances. However, there is a downside to this; insects are cold blooded, and their muscles will not function adequately until the body temperature is raised to over 30° C. Butterflies gain heat by basking in the sun, but night-flying moths have to warm up by shivering their wings, generating heat by the rapid muscle contractions. Especially if the air is cold, shivering may take several minutes. Imagine now a bird that has discovered a death's head moth, resting on a tree in the early morning. The moth cannot fly – its only way out is to change its form and reappear to the bird in a different guise. When it opens its wings the bright yellow and black pattern that earned it the name of 'Bee Tiger' amongst the Aurelians is displayed on the body and hindwings, displacing the dull bark-like colour of the folded forewings:

> This weird skull-marked fearsome moth
> Is just a sheep in wolf-like cloth
> The devil's in the detail now
> Neither fish nor fowl somehow
> An entomological transvestite
> An insect tiger burning bright
> I wish I had a skill like this
> To defend by metamorphosis
> Setting the cat among the pige-ones
> With a little image of human bones.

(Author)

The deception is compounded by the tiger stripes that signify wasps and hornets, which a bird is much more likely to encounter than it is a tiger, but apart from the striped abdomen the resemblance ceases – or does it? I puzzled over this and kept returning to the conundrum for many years. My eureka moment came when I was giving a talk about insect mimicry in my local village. I had loaded my slide of the moth upside-down in error and suddenly saw an image that I recalled having seen in Walter Linsenmaier's (1917–2000) superbly illustrated book *Insects of the World* (1972). It was the cream-coloured head capsule of a Japanese giant hornet, *Vespa mandarinia*. Like everyone else, I had pored over specimens and photographs of the death's head moth in the head-up position, ignoring the fact that a bird or lizard would be most likely to see the moth from a quite different perspective, low down, facing the moth more or less head-on. From this position the skull mark becomes a hornet's head, attached to the striped abdomen (Figs. 18 & 19). The crossbones become the pale segments of the base of the antennae whilst the dark orbits become the compound eyes. The little triangle of three simple eyes is seen between the antennal inserts, the upper lip is the crown of the 'skull' with the black pointed tips of the mandibles imprinted on it[24].

---

[24] See Howse, 2010

Hornets are dangerous creatures. The Japanese giant hornet, sometimes known as the Asian giant hornet (Fig. 19), rejoices in vernacular names such as 'yak killer', 'giant sparrow bee' and 'tiger head bee', and in magazine articles often as 'the hornet from hell'; it is one of the most unpleasant and terrifying insects you could wish to meet. It is reported that, on average, forty people die every year in Japan of anaphylactic shock after having been stung, which makes the Japanese giant hornet the most lethal animal in that country (bears kill zero to five people and venomous snakes kill five to ten people each year).

This hornet has a sting that is 6 mm long, and the sensation of a sting is said to be like a red-hot nail driven into the skin. Not only that but it sends out scouts that call in their nest mates with pheromone when they locate a bees' nest, and they all have powerful mandibles that they use to tear honeybees, on which they prey, from limb to limb. One hornet can slaughter around forty bees. Any sentient bee would have empathised with the experience of Odysseus and his men when they arrived in Laestrygonia[25]:

> [Antiphates] prepared my crew a barbarous welcome.
> Snatching one of my men, he tore him up for dinner …
> That brought tremendous Laestrygonians swarming up
> From every side – hundreds, not like men, like Giants!
> …
> They speared the crews like fish
> And whisked them home to make their grisly meal.

What better icon could there be – what more threatening flag to fly to keep enemies of moths at bay than the image of a giant hornet? The yellow and black stripe pattern (which we also see plastered as a warning on scaffolding, road barriers and emergency vehicles) is one which has evolved perhaps thousands of times in harmless hoverflies as an *aide-mémoire* to potential predators, a predictor of possible dire consequences if they are seized. This is the form of mimicry known as 'Batesian' after the intrepid naturalist Henry Walter Bates (see Chapter 3) (1892).

---

[25] Homer, The Odyssey, transl. Robert Fagles

The lesser death's head moth, *Acherontia styx*, overlaps in distribution with the Asian hornet, *Vespa velutina*, which has similar predatory habits to its Japanese cousin. In Europe and the Near East there are other possible mimicry models for *A. atropos*, which include other hornet species and (non-social) scoliid wasps such the mammoth wasp, *Megascolia maculata* (Fig. 20). The latter is the largest wasp in Europe which has a powerful sting and preys on the larvae of rhinoceros beetles.

It is a great conceit of humans to think that a moth or butterfly looks the same to every animal as it does to us. The scientist, artist, graphic designer, poet and peasant alike, all pore over objects from Etruscan vases to the daily newspaper and the smallest flea, making sure they are seeing them the 'right way up'. But why should we assume that animals that don't have their feet on the ground much of the time, as we do, but rather forage up and down among branches at every inclination to the vertical do that? I started looking at living butterflies and moths upside-down and found faces of owls, bird beaks and heads, fox, lizard, rodent and frog faces. I then looked for other images embedded in the wings margins and discovered snakes, caterpillars, salamanders, spiders, beetles and millipedes. The discoveries seemed never ending. I described many of them in my book *Butterflies: Messages from Psyche*, expecting a chorus of skeptical comments about what you can see in inkblots if you try. It was a pleasant surprise to find that only one person wrote to me in the latter vein, but dozens of people were intrigued to have been shown the way to interpret the messages on the wings of butterflies and moths and have started to look at things the 'wrong way up'. The examples of this form of mimicry, which I have called 'satyric', have proven too numerous to ignore or put down to chance. The crucial point to recognise is that the ambiguity of the image causes confusion in the eyes of a predator. If it really is a hornet, a mouthful could be lethal. Just a few thousandths of a second of hesitation by a predator gives potential insect prey an opportunity to run away, fall or call on emergency energy reserves and fly a short distance[26].

Originally, this chapter ended here, but then I found a live death's head moth to photograph. To my astonishment I discovered that

---

[26] See also Howse, 2013

there were two more images that I and everyone else had overlooked. Driving through France, from time to time you come across a notice at unmanned railway crossings 'UN TRAIN PEUT EN CACHER UN AUTRE'. If you pay too much attention to the first train then you may ignore the possibility that there is another one just behind it. The second train in this case is an image very like that of a sparrow. You didn't notice it the first time you saw an image of the moth, I suspect, and neither did I. It is outlined in Fig. 21: a bird's head, yellow eyes and beak, outstretched wings and claws, very like a sparrow. Nestlings of small birds are primed to the parents departing and returning, folding their wings as they land. The third 'train' was captured in a photograph in which the moth when threatened raises both front black hairy legs in a salute (Fig. 22, left). This is a defence posture found in some wolf and tarantula spiders (Fig. 22, right), but what makes it particularly intriguing here is that the legs of many tarantula species have colour rings on them, sometimes yellow ones at the bases of each leg joint. More in evidence are the bright yellow, tufted cushions beneath the head which can be expanded as part of the display of the moth, but which may be copies of the ornamentation of the powerful *chelicerae* (poison jaws) of lycosid wolf spiders. Jean-Henri Fabre (1823–1915), who popularised the study of entomology in the early part of the twentieth century in his beautifully written accounts of his encounters with invertebrates, described (1912) the hunting behaviour of the wolf spider, the so-called Narbonne Lycosa, *Lycosa narbonensis*, which can leap into the air to bring down insect prey as large as dragonflies and locusts and sink its fangs into them.

The death's head hawk-moth, a creature we see as just another moth, although a weird one at that, I now suggest is a chimaera. But while it may seem that to us, to a bird it is a great illusionist, or rather there are a number of things it could be, if, as I have argued, birds have no, or limited, Gestalt imagery but identify other animals by elementary sign stimuli. Thus, like the Hindu God Brahma, the moth is four-headed, each head giving a separate message: hornet, sparrow, wolf spider and squeaking mouse. It is in the same category as the duck-billed platypus, *Ornithorhynchus anatinus*, which is a creature, as Umberto Eco (1932–2016) maintained (2000), with several referents: a duck bill, otter feet, fur, a tail like that of a beaver, milk glands, a creature which is egg-laying and amphibious with a reptilian gait. It took 86 *years* before the various ambiguities of this animal were resolved by systematicians and before it was determined that the platypus was neither bird, nor beaver, nor amphibian, nor placental mammal. By comparison, any insect that could, by its ambiguous appearance, confuse a potential vertebrate predator for 86 milliseconds would have an excellent chance of survival. Ambiguity is the driving force in the evolution of mimicry.

This chapter would not be complete if we did not now take another look at *A. lachesis* and *A. styx* (Fig. 9). Again, *A. lachesis*, the greater death's head moth, has a skull-like marking on the thorax, used to justify its name; but is that what it is? Examine the photograph in Fig. 23 of the insect head-down and you may recognise the nose and nostrils of a mammal, the glint of two small eyespots on the folded wings and the suggestion of ears on the wing tips. Seen head-up (Fig. 21), on the other hand, the image of a giant hornet dominates, as in all three moths. *A. lachesis* is likewise a chimaera: nature has created for birds, reptiles and other vertebrate insectivores what is the equivalent of a dragon for us, neither one thing nor another.

9

MIRRORS TO REALITY

Why is a butterfly bluer than blue?
Whiter than white? I wish I knew
Wavelength, sharp refraction of light
Laws of Physics get it right
Micro-structure tells you why.
Photons make a butterfly

Why is a moth rose-red as the dawn
Coloured with soft velvet hues wing-borne?
The answer's there in Chemistry:
Bio-synthetic wizardry
Melanic pigments tell you why.
Molecules make a butterfly.

Why are designs in wings perceived:
Patterns no artist has ever conceived?
Natural selection is the means
Survival of blind, selfish genes
DNA helices tell you why.
Mutations make a butterfly

What use is a molecule or photon-
Or instructions DNA will pass on,
To Homer or Michelangelo?

Would it help any artist to know?
What makes beauty on an insect's wing?
What strange muse makes the heart sing?

(Author)

In 1978 the Estonian composer Arvo Pärt composed a beautiful piece of music which has become one of the most popular modern works on the world scene. The composition is based on minimalism, including triads of notes that are regularly repeated but with small changes each time, and a repetitive melody that ends alternately on ascending and descending notes. He called this 'Spiegel im Spiegel', or 'mirrors within a mirror', referring to the reflections of light between two parallel mirrors. When an image between the two mirrors is reflected from one mirror to the other, it creates a new image further away but one which is changed. It is perceived at a greater distance, is reversed from left to right and becomes progressively smaller and fainter as the reflections multiply, continuing theoretically to sub-atomic dimensions. This represents in some respects the process of science in the search for ultimate causes, which goes into greater and greater detail, each successive level solving one question but creating another, taking us further away from what we perceive with our unaided senses into an increasingly microscopically dissected world. Ultimately, we have to return in order to understand what is for us the 'real world' around us again – a view famously expressed by Thomas S. Eliot (1888–1965) in his poem *The Waste Land*:

We shall not cease from exploration and the end of all our exploring will be to arrive where we started and know the place for the first time.

Some writers, including Jonah Lehrer (2012), have argued that fundamental truths about human existence are revealed by art and literature as much as by science. Recent studies in neuroscience help us to understand why this is so. Evidence has been found for two different neural networks in the brain, two brains within a brain. One network becomes active when someone is carrying out an analytical task or work out the answer to a problem. The other comes into play when we are engaged in social interactions that demand empathy. Just as we cannot see the faces and the vase at the same time in the well-known Rubin's vase illusion, because the perception of one inhibits perception of the other, so the theoretical physicist must stop thinking of the mathematic constructs underlying the behaviour of elementary particles in order to enjoy the flowers in his garden. It has also been shown that too much devotion to analytical thinking discourages religious belief (2012), something that Buddhist philosophers have long known.

Rubin's vase illusion

The neuroscientist Anthony I. Jack (2013) explains:

> We see neural inhibition between the entire brain network we use to socially, emotionally and morally engage with others, and the entire network we use for scientific, mathematical and logical reasoning.
>
> This shows scientific accounts really do leave something out – the human touch. A major challenge for the science of the mind is how we can better translate between the cold and distant mechanical descriptions that neuroscience produces, and the emotionally engaged intuitive understanding which allows us to relate to one another as people.

The intuitive part of the brain is regarded by some neurologists as a means of providing a shortcut to perception and understanding of the world around us. The perceptions of artists, novelists and poets have been expressed in their works, and in every culture in the world they have been enshrined in mythology and allegory. Myths provide relief maps of the routes of thought that, unconsciously, we tend to follow when we encounter something new or unusual or try to make sense of events. The French anthropologist and ethnologist, Claude Lévi-Strauss (1908–2009), the father of Structuralism, has argued that myths play an important role in conceptual thinking. He compared myths from tribes from Chile to the Arctic Circle, showing that, although the stories might be very different, the underlying structure is very similar, involving a confrontation of opposites and a resolution through an intermediary. The myth of Theseus and the Minotaur, for example, involved a confrontation between a heroic figure and a monster, resolved with the help of Ariadne's golden thread.

What is in the myth is usually neither true from a scientific point of view nor possible in the world as we know it but provides a kind of mental scaffolding around which new tendrils of thought grow, flowering into brief periods of new understanding that enable us not only to construct our own reality but also to be creative. Lévi-Strauss expressed this by saying that 'myths get thought in man unbeknownst to him'. He explained the differences between the scientific approach and that of non-scientists as follows (2012):

> The work of the painter, the poet or the musician, like the myths and symbols of the savage, ought to be seen by us, if not as a superior form of knowledge, at least as the most fundamental and the only one really common to us all; scientific thought is merely the sharp point – more penetrating because it has been whetted on the stone of fact, but at the cost of some loss of substance –and its effectiveness is to be explained by its power to pierce sufficiently deeply for the main body of the tool to follow the head.

Taking this as a starting point, we can now see how the Greek myth of Perseus and the Medusa gives insights into the patterns of thought that we follow in our perception of the death's head moth. The essence of this is that the mask of the Medusa not only resembles the 'skull' of the death's head but was also used for protection. The Gorgon Medusa, the legend goes, was so frightening in appearance that men and animals that saw her face and looked into her eyes were instantly turned to stone, and when Perseus sought her out, the land around was strewn with petrified bodies of men and animals.

The Ashmolean Museum in Oxford is home, among many other wonderful things, to some magnificent ancient Greek and Roman sculptures. As I walked through the gallery, it was difficult not to feel I was being watched by these silent men, women and gods that, like the casualties of the Medusa, had been instantaneously petrified in past millennia. And then, suddenly in front of me was the head of the Gorgon. It is carved on a marble bust with a head of Roman origin that is clearly of different stone (Fig. 24). The head has been spliced on to the breast and dates to 25–150 AD, but the bust is much later, 1600–1750 AD, and bears a Medusa head on the breastplate, bringing to mind the parallel image of the skull on the thorax of the moth.

The Gorgons were three sisters, Stheno, Euryale and Medusa. The Gorgon Medusa[27] was the only sister who was mortal. She was of fearsome appearance with snakes for hair. Ovid, though, in his *Metamorphoses* says that the Medusa was once a lovely woman:

> She was once most beautiful in form, and the jealous hope of many suitors. Of all her beauties, her hair was the most beautiful – for so I learned from one who said he had seen her. 'Tis said that in Minerva's temple Neptune, lord of the Ocean, ravished her. Jove's daughter turned away and hid her chaste eyes behind her aegis. And, that the deed might be punished as was due, she changed the Gorgon's locks to ugly snakes. And now to frighten her fear-numbed foes, she still wears upon her breast the snakes which she has made.

The Gorgons were highly dangerous, but only the Medusa was mortal, and Perseus undertook the task of killing her. He was helped by the goddess Athena who sent him to the west of the world, known to the ancient Greeks as the Hesperides (probably in Libya). There he found the Stygian nymphs that provided him with the equipment necessary to accomplish his mission: a sack in which he could keep the Medusa's head safely, an adamantine scimitar and a pair of

---

[27] Ovid, *Metamorphoses* Book IV: vs. 791-803

winged sandals. Hades, the refuge for souls of the dead in ancient Greek mythology, was ruled by the god of the same name. He had a helmet of invisibility, which he lent to Perseus who used it in his quest to kill the Medusa.

Perseus knew he stood no chance of success if he met the gaze of the Medusa. Great power was ascribed to the eye in Greek mythology, and even today belief in the evil eye still persists in the eastern Mediterranean and parts of Asia. Removing the eyes also has powerful symbolism, enacted in Gloucester in *King Lear* by Shakespeare and in *Oedipus the King* by Sophocles, leaving the victim powerless as a punishment for his own unseeing acts.

Perseus, however, rather than blinding the Medusa set out to behead her so that her deadly gaze could be preserved and turned to his own advantage. He found the Gorgons asleep and, using the reflection in Athena's shield to avoid looking into the eyes of the Medusa, he then severed her head and placed it safely in the magic bag. He avoided the pursuit of the sisters by donning his helmet of invisibility. On his journey towards Egypt, Perseus turned unfriendly characters to stone on the way by bringing the head of Medusa out of its bag, creating, for example, the Atlas Mountains from the recumbent giant Atlas. He eventually came across the beautiful nymph Andromeda chained to rocks on a cliff, where for her misdemeanours she had been placed by her family to be devoured by a sea monster. It was love at first sight; Perseus killed the sea monster with his scimitar and petrified his rival suitor and companions by lifting his Medusa head again out of its bag.

The archaeologist Marija Gimbutas traced the origin of the Medusa mask in Europe to around 600 BC, concluding that it was seen as both deadly and regenerative (like alcohol consumed in symposia[28] perhaps). This view she supported with a quotation from Apollodorus that one drop of blood from the Medusa's hair-snakes caused instant death but a second brought life and rebirth. We can suppose that the Medusa head (Fig. 26) was intended in most instances to keep evil spirits at bay, a conclusion that is reinforced on the ceramic by images on the reverse side of four eyes (no doubt designed to repel the evil eye), intertwined snakes and, at the base, a penis and testicles (discreetly inverted in the museum display cabinet, perhaps to avoid

---

[28] The name given to convivial drinking parties in ancient Greece

shocking the less prurient). In Roman times the penis was also used to repel the evil eye, like a forceful kind of two-fingered salute to evil spirits, and was found on mosaic floors and on street corners – as in Pompeii for example. Each eye is placed on the outline of a bird's head, possibly because birds, along with scorpions and dogs, were also considered enemies of the evil eye. The image of two intertwined snakes suggests the emblem of Asclepias, the ancient Greek god of medicine (snakes were used in healing rituals).

The process of demonising the Medusa involved her portrayal with archetypal features of wild animals that have posed serious threats to man since the origin of the human race. The Gorgons all had writhing snakes for hair, the canine teeth and a broad protruding tongue of a large carnivore, a round, simian-type face with large, round, staring eyes with black pupils, and huge wings of shining gold and claws of bronze. These wild, fierce animal characteristics, built into the gargoyles that our ancestors used to protect churches, also figure in the allegorical masterpiece which is Dante's (1265–1321) *Devine Comedy*. On his journey to the underworld, Dante was confronted by a lion, a leopard and a she-wolf, said to represent some of the worst aspects of human nature. Eventually he crossed the river Acheron and entered hell where he encountered the devil.

Satan, like the Gorgon Medusa, is considered by some to have once been a perfect being. On trying to usurp God, he was thrown out of heaven and condemned to live in hell for eternity, transformed into the demonic state, like the Gorgons, as a giant with three heads, spiny bat wings, horns, body fur or scales and sharp metal claws (the connection with dragons is very plain).

On his journey into hell, Dante meets the Furies of hell, equally repulsive, which frighten the living daylights out of him[29]:

> …stained with blood; who had the limbs and attitude of women and were girt with greenish hydras: for hair, they had little serpents and cerastes [vipers] wherewith their horrid temples were bound.

---

[29] Dante, *The Devine Comedy*, Inferno Canto IX:34-63 The Furies (Conscience) and Medusa (Obduracy)

> With their claws each was rending her breast; they were smiting themselves with their palms, and crying so loudly, that I pressed close to the poet for fear. 'Let Medusa come, that we may change him to stone,' they all said, looking downwards…
> Dante's guide replies:
> 'Turn thee backwards, and keep thy eyes closed; for if the Gorgon shew herself, and thou shouldst see her, there would be no returning up again.'

The power that accrued to Gorgon-type images has led, in many cultures throughout the world, to the belief that the power could be harnessed to enhance the survival of their societies by appeasement of what became terrible gods, leading to idols, offerings, sacrifice and ritual worship. Bernal Diaz del Castillo (1492–1582) was the last survivor from among the followers of Hernán Cortéz (1485–1547), famous Spanish conquistador and explorer. Before he died Diaz wrote his enthralling first-hand account of *The Conquest of New Spain*. The conquistadors of Mexico turned their backs on the god Tezcatlipoca, the Aztec equivalent of the Furies, who held the Aztecs in a thrall that they propitiated constantly with human sacrifices. Diaz wrote (1974):

> We…saw another great image…with a face like a bear and eyes that glittered.…This Tezcatlipoca, the god of hell, had charge of the Mexicans' souls, and his body was surrounded by figures of little devils with snakes' tails. The walls of this shrine were so caked with blood and the floor so bathed in it that the stench was worse than any slaughterhouse in Spain.

In an intriguing parallel, many of these threatening medusoid features can be found in moths; images of canine teeth, claws, snake heads, owl eyes and so forth have recently been shown to exist in many species of butterfly and giant silk-moths (Howse, 2015). The death's head moth, for example, shares many features of the Medusa. It has golden wings (the undersides of all the wings are a golden yellow colour) and the skull mark can also be seen as a white face with two large black orbits. Perseus's 'cloak of invisibility' lent to him by Hades also brings to mind the moth's ability to escape detection by bees (Fig. 17).

The mask of the Medusa became a fascination of many artists, Michelangelo Caravaggio (1571–1610) prominent among them. He revealed his tortured and violent soul in some of his paintings: several included severed heads, for example *The Beheading of John the Baptist*, *Judith Beheading Holofernes* and *Salome Receives the Head of St John the Baptist*. In 1576, he and his family left Milan to avoid the plague, and in 1592 he had to flee from there to Rome after he had been involved in various street fights in which a policeman had been injured. In the years leading up to his violent death in 1610 the Pope issued a death warrant for him after he committed a murder.

In 1598–99, during his period in Rome, Caravaggio was commissioned to paint the *Head of the Medusa* for the Grand Duke of Tuscany. The painting was done on wood and the head was portrayed on a bronze shield (Fig. 25). The image he created has extra power because it captures the Medusa at the moment of her death, but many believe it to be a self-portrait (leaving the snakes aside), in which case Caravaggio becomes the powerful Medusa head made from his own reflection in the bronze shield. Could he have been picturing himself as safe only as a reflected image but otherwise highly dangerous? The Medusa's power is turned into a symbol, in a way not too dissimilar from that in which Christ's image survives as a cross, a powerful symbol behind which, amongst others, the Spanish Conquistadors and the Knights Templar marched.

An alternative interpretation of Caravaggio's Medusa is that it alludes to an anecdote about Leonardo de Vinci[30].

Leonardo's father acquired a buckler (small shield) made from the wood of a fig tree and asked his son to paint something on it. Leonardo polished and shaped the wood…And afterwards… he began to think what he could paint upon it, that might be able to terrify all who should come upon it, producing the same effect as once did the head of Medusa. For this purpose, then, Leonardo carried to a room of his own into which no one entered save himself alone, lizards great and small, crickets, serpents, butterflies, grasshoppers, bats, and other

---

[30] *Vita di Leonardo* In: Vasari, 1568

strange kinds of suchlike animals (some of these animals he dissected), out of the number of which, variously put together, he formed a great ugly creature, most horrible and terrifying, which emitted a poisonous breath and turned the air to flame; and he made it coming out of a dark and jagged rock, belching forth venom from its open throat, fire from its eyes, and smoke from its nostrils, in so strange a fashion that it appeared altogether a monstrous and horrible thing; and so long did he labour over making it, that the stench of the dead animals in that room was past bearing, but Leonardo did not notice it, so great was the love that he bore towards art.

Ser Piero,[the father] at the first glance, taken by surprise, gave a sudden start, not thinking that that was the buckler, nor merely the [painted] form that he saw upon it, and, falling back a step, Leonardo checked him, saying, 'This work serves the end for which it was made; take it, then, and carry it away, since this is the effect that it was meant to produce.'

What Leonardo had obviously done was to create a mythical animal similar to the basilisk, and he did in fact make a sketch of that creature. According to Pliny the Elder (23–79 BC) (1991), the basilisk 'is a snake with a light crown upon its head. It suffocates bushes not only through its touch but also by breathing on them and it crunches stones; such is the evil, spiteful power of the animal'.

The glance of the basilisk was said to be lethal, but it could be killed by the smell of weasels, the crowing of a cockerel or the sight of its reflection in a mirror. The power of the basilisk was known to Alexander the Great (356–323 BC). When a thousand of his soldiers died, he believed that they had encountered a basilisk. Francis Bacon (1623) tells us that he subsequently made use of a mirror to defeat one:

'... [glass] bodies could be so shaped that poisonous and infectious species and influences could be directed wherever a man might want. For thus Aristotle is said to have taught Alexander, who by this teaching directed the poison of the basilisk erected on the city wall against his army back into the city itself.'

On seeing its reflection, the monster died instantly. Alexander also made use of an image of the Medusa's head. In the Neapolitan National Museum of Archaeology there is a magnificent mosaic (constructed using one and a half million tesserae), dating from around 100 BC, which came from the House of the Faun in Pompeii (Fig. 28). It is a scene from a battle between the armies of Alexander and King Darius III of Persia in which Alexander on horseback, focusing his gaze on Darius, is depicted with the mask of the Medusa on his breastplate. This appears to have done the trick: Alexander defeated Darius in this and one further battle a few years later.

This myth of the Medusa is believed by some historians to represent the history of warfare between the peoples of the eastern Mediterranean in coded form. According to the second century, Greek geographer Pausanius (*c.* 110–*c.* 180 AD), the myth of the Gorgons derives from a race of 'wild' men and women in the Lybian desert around Lake Tritonius who harassed the neighbouring populations until their leader, Medusa, was killed by Perseus.

In the valley of Roncal in northern Spain the nobleman's heraldic shield, to which all the men in the valley are entitled, bears an image of the severed head of the Emir Abderramán (731–788 AD), the powerful Moorish ruler of Córdoba. He took his army north as far as Toulouse in 786 and returned through Aragon intent on persecuting the Roncalese. During the unequal battle that followed, the King of Navarre arrived unexpectedly with his soldiers and the Moors were routed. Abderramán was captured and beheaded by the women of Roncal.

There is at least one other heraldic shield with severed heads of Moors in Spain. The continued use of such symbols is, not unexpectedly, very controversial and is defended generally because it is a long-standing piece of social history. It teaches us, however, that the myth of Perseus and the Medusa could have arisen from a very similar event in the history of ancient Greece. The horror of such events has become enshrined symbolically in images of severed heads.

Significantly, in both the Gorgons and Lucifer the fallen angel, beauty is corrupted by archetypal features which are symbolic of fear and life-threatening encounters. This signifies that the transmogrified being, now regarded as ugly, can or must be killed. In this process of dehumanisation we see here the roots of prejudice, inter-racial violence and genocide. Demonisation also sheds light on what we regard as beauty. In the late 1960s the American ethologist Theodore C. Schneirla (1902–68) developed his Approach-Withdrawal theory of animal behaviour, which in more recent years has stimulated research in the field of human psychology. He was expressing a view that can be traced back to ancient mysticism in the near East. His thesis was that animals – young ones in particular – tend to avoid irregular stimuli: harsh discordant sounds, flickering light, unpredictable sudden movement etc., but were likely to approach melodious flute-like tones, unchanging patterns of light or colour and gentle movement. The latter are mostly associated with stability, safety of the home, parental care and so forth, while the former are associated with threatening predators. One path leads to contentment and (in humans) perceived beauty, the other to fear and alarm, where the concept of beauty goes out of the window and we then find ourselves treading the same seesaw of opposites that cannot co-exist in our minds at the same moment: love and hate, yin and yang, pleasure and pain, truth and falsehood. When looking at the image of the illusory Greek vase and the two profiles of the human head facing each other, or to look at a lovely woman with snakes in her hair or vampire teeth, or a beautiful insect marked with a skull and crossbones, the ambiguity torments us and stalls the thought process in the same way that it does the paradoxical contradiction when we consider the egregious slogans of the Party in George Orwell's (1903–50) influential satirical novel *Nineteen Eighty-Four* (1949):

War is peace. Freedom is slavery. Ignorance is strength.

According to some versions, Perseus gave the Medusa's head to the goddess Athena, who had it inserted on her breastplate. In the *Aeneid*, Virgil describes it as '—a fearsome thing with a surface of gold like scaly snakeskin … with serpents and the Gorgon herself upon the goddess's breast—a severed head rolling its eyes'. It was a weapon with which to transfix her enemies in fear. In an historical context, the inclusion of this icon on statues of the goddess in Athens would have served as a symbol of the military power of the city and its patron goddess.

The British war poet Robert Graves (1895–1985) maintained that the ægis (the name given to the Gorgon image or its container) was 'a magical goatskin bag containing a serpent, and protected by a Gorgon mask'(1955) and noted that Herodotus identified the source of the ægis as Libya, which was always a distant territory of ancient enchantment for the ancient Greeks[31]:

> Athene's garments and ægis were borrowed by the Greeks from the Libyan women, who are dressed in exactly the same way, except that their leather garments are fringed with thongs, not serpents.

In Ancient Greece, a *Gorgoneion* – a representation of a Gorgon face, often with snakes a protruding tongue and vampiric teeth, was put on armour, buildings and tombstones to repel evil spirits, thus offering an interesting parallel with the Stinsford grave (Chapter 1). There is also a comparison to be made with the fearsome-looking protective goddess Kali of Hindu mythology, who has a reputation for devouring her foes. She is often shown with a protruding tongue and snakes around her head and is commonly pictured as an icon carrying a severed head. The ancient Chinese rattan shields, used by foot soldiers to deflect the blows of swords, commonly had a tiger face painted on them to intimidate the opponent. These faces closely resembled the Medusae of the Greek aegis (Fig. 27).

Sigmund Freud used the Greek concept of the Underworld (also called *Hades* or '*Acheronta*' by various authors) as a model for his concept of the unconscious, which he viewed as a repository of repressed fears and desires. His method of psychoanalysis expounded in his seminal work *The Interpretation of Dreams* was based on recovery and confrontation of the forgotten memories and traumas in which he quoted a line from Virgil's Aeneid: '*flectere si nequeo superos, Acheronta movebo*', rendered by the poet John Dryden (1631–1700) as:

> If Jove and Heav'n my just desires deny,
> Hell shall the pow'r of Heav'n and Jove supply.

---

[31] Herodotus (*c.* 484–*c.* 425 BC) *Histories* IV.189

In *Das Medusenhaupt* (*Medusa's Head*) Freud (1922) drew again on Greek mythology to explain the significance of the Medusa. He linked the severed head to the female genitalia, the sight of which he suggested fed a young boy's castration complex and, at the same time, the conflict of imagery tended to stimulate an erection. With characteristic speculative bravado, Freud saw the Medusa's petrification skills as a metaphor for this, one that was later seized upon by the psychologist Ronald D. Laing (1927–89) (1960): 'Freud was a hero. He descended to the Underworld and met there stark terrors. He carried with him his theory as a Medusa's head which turned these terrors to stone.'

In 1932, shortly before the Second World War, Einstein and Freud exchanged correspondence which was published under the title *Why War?* This publication came to be banned in Hitler's Germany, and the two great men were driven into exile. In the exchange, Freud discussed the opposing tendencies ('instincts' in his terminology) in human nature for destruction and social co-operation and love, claiming that these can become unbalanced and the destructive instinct can be fed by energy from the unconscious. As we have seen, Freud drew his concepts, which he admitted were themselves mythological in nature, from the Greek myths. He laid challenge to the view that ultimately mythology would give way to science:

> Does not every science come in the end to a kind of mythology like this? Cannot the same be said today of your physics?

Einstein avoided answering these questions directly but expressed admiration for Freud's philosophy:

> When I wrote you I was thoroughly convinced of the insignificance of my role, which was only meant to document my good will, with me as the bait on the hoof; to tempt the marvellous fish into nibbling. You have given in return something altogether magnificent.

Freud's views came to the fore on George Orwell's *Nineteen Eighty-Four*, which pictures the dystopian state controlled by Big Brother, the figurehead of the Party, which has the aim of bending perception and thought of individuals into total subservience. The ultimate torture applied to the unfortunate civil servant is confinement to the notorious room 101: exposure to the creatures of the underworld – snakes, spiders and ferocious rats – imprisoned around his head. This is an echo of the destructive forces of Freud's unconscious which were used to subvert the Eros instinct of the unfortunate Winston Smith and eradicate his love for his Julia and his fellow man.

In subtle contrast, Pablo Picasso's (1881–1973) *Guernica* harnesses the power of the unconscious as a weapon against fascism and war. None of the people or animals are faithfully portrayed in his monumental work which expresses the horror of mass carnage, but quasi-symbolic jagged images of teeth, horns, distorted bodies with open mouths and outstretched hands form a scene that does not need to have photographic realism to have intense numinous power.

The death's head moth with its fake skull can take us to the door of Room 101, and to Guernica, stirring the horrific images in our unconscious and changing our perception of a beautiful moth, invoking images of deadly diseases, death, tombstones and killing fields everywhere in the world. These concrete images that seethe in our unconscious have largely replaced the mystical ones of witches, evil spirits, devils, vengeful deities and Gorgons that dominated the lives, thoughts and feelings of man until the scientific enlightenment was well under way. But they are still latent within us and contribute to one of the many facets of the amorphous crystal of reality.

In his discussion on *Appearance and Reality, a chapter in The Problems of Philosophy* (1912), Bertrand Russell (1872–1970) argued that no two people experience a table – its colour, shape, texture, smell and the sounds it makes when rapped – in exactly the same way. The perception of each person is unique, depending upon what our senses tell us, and it is merely the appearance that we are aware of, not the true reality (if such exists). It is plain from the foregoing that what is already in the mind of the observer adds considerably to the uniqueness of individual perception. As in the philosophical approach to understanding perception, this, in Russell's words, allows us to ask questions 'which increase the interest of the world, and show the strangeness and wonder lying just below the surface'.

―――――

Image will show me everything
That my senses generate in me
Of the infinite and of the unique,
For which I eagerly seek.

To read such pictorial writing
Will make my life forever worthwhile
Then the Eternal, and the Being
I know will dwell within me.

From Herman Hesse, *Bekenntnis* (Faith)
(Author's Translation)

BIBLIOGRAPHY

Abram, David (1997). *The Spell of the Sensuous: Perception and Language in a More-Than-Human World*, Vintage Books, Penguin, London.

Allen, Keith (2009). Inter-species variation in colour perception. *Philosophical Studies* **142**: 197–220.

Bacon, Francis (1623). *De Dignitate et Augmentis Scientiarum libros IX*. Haviland, London.

Barber, Jesse R. & Kawahara, Akito Y. (2013). Hawkmoths produce anti-bat ultrasound. *Biology Letters* **9**: 20130161.

Baron-Cohen, Simon & Harrison, John E. (eds.) (1997). *Synaesthesia: Classic and Contemporary Readings*, Wiley-Blackwell, Oxford.

Bates, Henry Walter (1892). *A Naturalist on the River Amazons,* John Murray, London.

Bromenshenk, Jerry *et al.* (2003). Can honeybees assist in area reduction and landmine detection? *The Journal of Mine Action* **7** (3).

Busnel, R.-G. & Dumortier, Bernard (1959). Vérification par des méthodes d'analyse acoustique des hypothèses sur l'origine du cri du Sphinx *Acherontia atropos* (Linné), *Bulletin de la Société entomologique de France* **64** (3–4): 44–58.

Butler, Colin G., Callow, Robert K. & Johnston, N. C. (1962). The isolation and synthesis of queen substance, 9-oxodec-trans-2-enoic acid, a honey-bee pheromone, *Proceedings of the Royal Society of London Series B Biological Sciences* **155** (960): 417–432.

Carroll, Lewis (1871). *Through the Looking Glass*, Macmillan, USA.

Classen, Constance (1992). The Smell Report, *Ethos* **20** (2): 133–66.

Classen, Constance; Howes, David & Synnott, Anthony (1994). *Aroma: The Cultural History of Smell.* Routledge, Abingdon.

Darwin, Charles (1859). *The Origin of Species*, John Murray, London.

Diaz, Bernal (1974). *The Conquest of New Spain*, transl. J.M. Cohen, Folio Society, London.

Dittrich, W. *et al.*, (1993). Imperfect mimicry - a pigeon's perspective, *Proceedings of the Royal Society of London Series B* **251**: 195–200.

Eco, Umberto (2000). *Kant and the Platypus: Essays on Language and Cognition*, transl. Alastair McEwen, Vintage Publishing, London.

Fabre, Jean-Henri (1912). *The Life of the Spider*, transl. Alexander Teixeira de Mattos, Hodder & Stoughton, London.

Fowles, John (1998). *The Nature of Nature*, reprinted in *Wormholes: Essays and occasional writings*, Jonathan Cape, London.

Frazer, James G. (1890). *The Golden Bough*, Macmillan and Co., London.

Gervais, Will M. & Norenzayan, Ara (2012). Analytic thinking promotes religious disbelief, *Science* **336** (6080): 493–496. doi: 10.1126/science.1215647.

Gimbutas, Marija (2001). *The Living Goddesses*, (ed. M. R. Dexter), University of California Press Ltd., USA.

Goethe, Johann Wolfgang von (1808). *Faust: Eine Tragödie*, Erster Teil, J.G. Cotta'schen Buchhandlung, Tübingen.

Göpfert, Martin C. & Wasserthal, Lutz T. (1999). Hearing with the mouthparts: Behavioural responses and the structural basis of ultrasound reception in acherontine hawkmoths. *Journal of Experimental Biology* **202**: 909–918.

Graves, Robert (1955). *The Greek Myths*, Penguin Books, London.

Graves, Robert (1961). *The White Goddess*, Faber, London.

Gregory, Richard L. & Wallace, Jean G. (1963). Recovery from Early Blindness: A Case Study, *Experimental Psychology Society Monograph* No. 2.

Grieve, Maud (1931). *A Modern Herbal*, Dover Publications, USA.

Grimaldi, David & Engel, Michael S. (2005). *Evolution of the Insects*, Cambridge University Press, UK.

Hardy, Thomas (1872). *Under the Greenwood Tree*, Tinsley Brothers, London.

Hardy, Thomas (1878). *The Return of the Native*, Belgravia, London.

Hertz, Ole (2001). Bambalutas – Death's Head Hawk Moth, *Bees for Development* No. 69.

Hesse, Hermann (1935). *Über Schmetterlinge* in *Falterschönheit*, Iris Verlag, Bern.

Hill, Susan (1970). *I'm the King of the Castle*, Hamish Hamilton, London.

Houghton, William (1888). *Sketches of British Insects – A Handbook for Beginners in the Study of Entomology*, Groombridge & Sons, London.

Howes, David (2006). Scent, Sound and Synaesthesia: Intersensoriality and Material Culture Theory. In: *Handbook of Material Culture*, Sage Publications, London.

Howse, Philip E. (2010). *Butterflies: messages from psyche*, Papadakis, London.

Howse, Philip E. (2013). Lepidopteran wing patterns and the evolution of satyric mimicry, *Biological Journal of the Linnean Society* **109:** 203–214.

Howse, Philip (2015). *Seeing Butterflies: New Perspectives on Colour Mimicry & Camouflage*, Papadakis, London.

Howse, Philip E. & Allen, John A. (1994). Satyric mimicry: the evolution of apparent imperfection, *Proceedings of the Royal Society of London Series B, Biological Sciences* **257**: 111–114.

Howse, Philip E. & Underwood, Karen L. (2000). Environmentally-safe pest control using novel bio-electrostatic techniques, In: *Area-wide control of Fruit Flies and other Insect Pests*, (ed. K.-H. Tan, Penerbit), University Sains Malaysia, Penang.

Huber, François (1796). *Nouvelles Observations sur les Abeilles*, Debray, Paris.

Huxley, Aldous L. (1932). *Brave New World*, Chatto & Windus, London.

Huxley, Aldous L. (1954). *The Doors of Perception*, Chatto & Windus, London.

Jack, Anthony I. *et al.* (2013). fMRI reveals reciprocal inhibition between social and physical cognitive domains, *Neuroimage* **66**: 385–401. doi: 10.1016/j.neuroimage.2012.10.061

Jameson, Kimberly A., Highnote, Susan M. & Wasserman, Linda M. (2001). Richer color experience in observers with multiple photopigment opsin genes, *Psychonomic Bulletin and Review* **8** (2): 244–261.

Jung, Carl G. (1960). *Synchronicity, an Acausal Connecting Principle*, Princeton University Press, USA.

Karlson, Peter & Lüscher, Martin (1959). 'Pheromones': a New Term for a Class of Biologically Active Substances, *Nature* **183** (4653): 55–56.

Kawahara, Akito Y. & Barber, Jesse R. (2015). Tempo and mode of antibat ultrasound and sonar jamming in the diverse hawkmoth radiation, *Proceedings of the National Academy of Sciences of the USA* **112** (20): 6407–6412.

Khayyám, Omar (1859). *Rubaiyat*, transl. Edward FitzGerald, Bernard Quaritch, UK.

Kiple, Kenneth F. & Ornelas, Kriemhild C. (eds.). (2000). *The Cambridge History of World Food*, Cambridge University Press, UK.

Kirby, William & Spence, William (1822–26). *An Introduction to Entomology*, Longman, Hurst, Rees, Orme & Brown, London.

Knapp, John L. (1853). *The Journal of a Naturalist*, John Murray, London.

Lack, David (1943). *The Life of the Robin*, H F & G Witherby, London.

Laing, Ronald D. (1960). *The Divided Self: An Existential Study in Sanity and Madness*, Penguin, Harmondsworth.

Land, Michael F. & Osorio, Daniel C. (2003). Colour vision: colouring the dark, *Current Biology* **13** (3): R83–5, doi.org/10.1016/S0960-9822(03)00031-9.

Lehrer, Jonah (2012). *Proust was a Neuroscientist*, Canongate Books, London.

Lévi-Strauss, Claude (2012). *Tristes Tropiques*, Chapter 13: Pioneer Zone, transl. Weightman, Penguin.

Linnaeus, Carl (1758). *Systema Naturae*, tenth Edition, Laurentius Salvius, Stockholm.

Linsenmaier, Walter (1972). *Insects of the World*. McGraw-Hill, New York.

Locke, John (1690). *An Essay Concerning Human Understanding*, Thomas Basset, London.

Lorenz, Konrad (1961). *King Solomon's Ring*, Methuen, London.

Lorenz, Konrad (1965). *Evolution and Modification of Behavior*, Chicago University Press.

Marren, Peter & Mabey, Richard (2010). *Bugs Britannica*, Chatto & Windus, London.

Melville, Herman (2012). *Moby Dick* (first published in 1851), Penguin, London.

Mollard-Desfour, Annie (2008). Les mots de couleur: des passages entre langues et cul-tures, *Synergies Italie*, no **4**: 23–32.

Moritz, Robin F. A., Kirchner, Wolfgang H. & Crewe, Robin M. (1991). Chemical camouflage of the death's head hawkmoth, (*Acherontia atropos* L.) in honeybee colonies, *Naturwissenschaften* **78** (4): 179–182.

Moseley, Henry N. (1872). On the sound made by the Death's Head Moth, "*Acherontia Atropos*", *Nature* **6**: 151–153.

Moss, Gloria (2014). *Why Men Like Straight Lines and Women Like Polka Dots: Gender and Visual Psychology*. Psyche Books, Winchester, UK.

Nabokov, Vladimir (1951). *Speak, Memory*, Victor Gollancz.

Nash, Robert J. *et al.* (1993). Calystegines in *Solanum* and *Datura* species and the death's-head hawk-moth (*Acherontia atropus*), *Phytochemistry* **34** (5): 1281–1283.

Okri, Ben (2007). *Starbook: A Magical Tale of Love and Regeneration*, Rider Books, London.

Orwell, George (1949). *Nineteen Eighty-Four: a novel*, Secker & Warburg, London.

Pavord, Anna (2004). *The Naming of Names: The Search for Order in the World of Plants*, Bloomsbury 2005, London.

Pliny the Elder (1991). *Natural History*, transl. John Healey, Penguin Classics.

Poe, Edgar Allen (1846). The Sphinx, *Arthur's Ladies' Magazine*, Philadelphia, USA.

Proust, Marcel (1931). *In Search of Lost Time III: The Guermantes Way*, Grasset & Gallimard, Paris.

Réaumur, René Antoine Ferchault de (1734–1742). *Mémoires pour servir á l'Histoire des Insectes*, L'Impremerie Royale, Paris.

Rupp, Robert M. (1991). Bee stings & their consequences, *The American Biology Teacher* **53** (5): 275–280.

Russell, Bertrand (1912). *The Problems of Philosophy*, Willams & Morgate, London.

Sacks, Oliver (1985). *The Man who Mistook his Wife for a Hat*, Summit Books, USA.

Sacks, Oliver (2012). *Hallucinations*, Knopf/Picador, New York.

Sales, Gillian & Pye, David (1974). *Ultrasonic communication by animals*, Chapman and Hall, London.

Sand, George (1873). *Impressions et Souvenirs*, Michel Lévy Frères, Paris.

Shlaer Robert (1972). An eagle's eye: quality of the retinal image. *Science* **176** (4037): 920–922.

Smith, Anthony (1971). *Mato Grosso*, Michael Joseph, London.

Stark, William S. (1987). Photopic sensitivities to ultraviolet and visible wavelengths and the effects of the macular pigments in human aphakic observers, *Current Eye Research* **6** (4): 631–638.

Stoker, Bram (1897). *Dracula*, Constable & Co, Edinburgh.

Swinton, Archibald H. (1880). *Insect Variety: its propagation and distribution*, Cassell, Petter, Galpin & Co, London, Paris, New York.

Tinbergen, Nikolaas (1951). *The Study of Instinct*, Oxford, Clarendon Press.

Ulanovsky, Nachum & Moss, Cynthia F. (2008). What the bat's voice tells the bat's brain, *Proceedings of the National Academy of Sciences of the USA* **105** (25): 8491–8498.

Vasari, Giorgio (1568). *Le vite de' più eccellenti pittori, scultori, e architettori*, Giunti, Florence.

Wallace, Alfred R. (1853). *A Narrative of Travels on the Amazon and Rio Negro with an Account of Native Tribes*, Ward Lock and Co., London.

Ward, Jamie (2008). *The Frog Who Croaked Blue: Synesthesia and the Mixing of the Senses,* Routledge, London.

Wilson, A. N. (2017). *Charles Darwin, Victorian Mythmaker.* John Murray, London.

Wood, John G. (1863). *The Illustrated Natural History*, Routledge, London.

Zeng, Jinyao *et al.* (2011). Moth wing scales slightly increase the absorbance of bat echolocation calls. *PLoS ONE* **6**(11): e27190. doi.org/10.1371/journal.pone.0027190.

Zhang, Fucheng *et al.* (2010). Fossilized melanosomes and the colour of Cretaceous dinosaurs and birds, *Nature* **463** (7284): 1075–1078.

INDEX